Trave

Cookie

Narrowboat Cruising with a Cat

David Thomas

Helen Krasner

ISBN: 1502385074
ISBN-13:978-1502385079

For Cookie,
and
boaters everywhere

Contents

Acknowledgements

Thanks are due to my mother and my sister Diane, who enabled my dream to become a reality. Thanks also to my son Josh, for spending time with me when he could have been out having fun, and for working countless locks and swing bridges (providing that it was in the afternoon), and to my daughter Lizzie for her constant support. I also owe a tremendous debt of gratitude to many people who have helped me along the way. I don't intend to make a list but you know who you are.

Foreword

In late 2009 I felt that I was at something of a crossroads in my life. For several years I had been working as a helicopter instructor and part time freelance writer, mainly writing about aviation for a number of magazines. It was an exciting and enjoyable way of life which I planned to continue for as long as I could. I lived in a lovely area of the Derbyshire Peak District with my much-loved cats, some of whom I used to show. I was happy and I had no plans for any drastic changes.

But life sometimes changes when you don't expect it to. My instructing work, which had actually been on the decline since the economic crash of 2007/8, began to dwindle even further. Then some of my writing work vanished too. I found myself working part time, mainly from home, and living in a very rural area where I didn't know that many people. For the first time I began to feel a bit lonely. I was single, and had been for many years. This had been fine when I was travelling and meeting people through my work – but that had now all but ceased. So my thoughts turned to perhaps finding someone to share my life with.

To be honest, this wasn't the first time I had felt this way. In fact, I had been frequenting the so-called 'dating' websites online for quite some time, usually in winter when I didn't manage to get airborne that often. However, I had been doing it more for fun and as a way of meeting people than with any serious intentions. Now, I began to think about trying harder.

So for the first time I enrolled on one of the paying sites rather than the free ones, which I'd been assured by those in the know were 'better' – and I chose the Guardian's site, 'Soulmates'.

Meeting a life partner at the age of 61 is probably never easy, and it is possibly particularly difficult when you have an unusual career plus several cats in tow. I met a few men, I went out with some, I made a few friends. But by early 2010 I had almost given up what I felt was a completely unrealistic idea. I let my Soulmates subscription lapse, only going on to the site occasionally, really just for something to do when I was web surfing.

Then one day I found something a little different – a profile written as though it was from a cat. I'd seen some profiles like this before of course; it's actually quite a common thing for cat lovers to do. But this one was different; it was well constructed, amusing, and grammatical. This last was important for me as a writer, trivial as it may seem to some. Anyway, the cat's 'boss' was five years younger than me, based in Tamworth which wasn't too far away, and lived on a narrowboat, which sounded intriguing and suggested that he might be an interesting person as well as a cat lover. Despite having pretty much given up hope, I had something of a hunch about this one.

The trouble was, my Soulmates subscription had lapsed, and I didn't feel like paying out good money to contact just one person, when past experience told me that he probably wouldn't prove to be anything special. Then, a few days later, Soulmates offered me a reduced short term subscription if I renewed. This seemed as though it might be a sign, so I re-joined. Then I wrote to David – or rather, I wrote as though from my Maine Coon cat, Magnus

We eventually met, and the rest, as they say, is history. Or rather, it is told in this book, from David's point of view, as this is his story. Over time I realised that David did have quite a story to tell. He had lived on a narrowboat with a cat for several years, cruising the waterways of England and Wales, which is fascinating in itself. Both he and the white fluffy Cookie-cat had had a number of hair-raising adventures. But his story also included bereavement, marriage breakup, loss of home, terminal diagnosis, severe depression...but finally romance, a seemingly miraculous recovery from illness, and a happy-ever-after type ending. I thought the whole account would make a wonderful book.

I had already written and published a travel/memoir type book. "Midges Maps & Muesli", published in 1998, is the story of a record breaking 5000 mile walk which I undertook around the coast of Britain in the 1980s. I had written numerous articles and a number of ebooks since that time, and also had two books on helicopter flying published. So I was well used to writing. I therefore suggested to David that we write the book together, and after some initial misgivings, he agreed. That is how "Travels With Cookie" came into being.

However, I should emphasise that the book is not ghost written! Initially I thought that perhaps it would be, but early on it became evident that David had definite ideas and his own way of putting things, which was nothing like mine. Gradually his own writing voice developed, and I simply helped with guidance, editing, and some general organisation. To summarise, we worked on it together as a team effort, but this is David's story. Everything in it really happened, but some names have been changed to protect people's privacy. We hope you enjoy reading it as much as we have enjoyed writing it.

Helen Krasner
August 2014

Prologue

What an idyllic day it was. After a leisurely breakfast I had set off in bright spring sunshine, boating down a small, peaceful canal, shaded by trees but with occasional rural views between them. This early in the year there were few holidaymakers, which meant hardly any other boaters were around. No-one was walking on the towpaths either, as it happened. This meant that the only noises were the throbbing of the boat's engine mixing with rural sounds from ducks, sheep and cows.

After about two hours I had moored close to a small town; later I would walk in there to check it out, explore and buy supplies for the next couple of days. But for now I was just sitting peacefully with a cup of tea, with my much-loved fluffy white cat, Cookie, on my knee. If things continued to be this quiet and there were no dogs around, I could safely let Cookie out to explore, keeping a careful eye on her of course. All was right with the world.

This was exactly how I had thought narrowboating would be, way back when I could only dream about living aboard a canal boat. But it wasn't always like this, as I now recalled. There were the numerous locks, tunnels, and swing bridges - although they had their own attraction and I rather enjoyed negotiating them. But there had also been the endless wet days, the cold days, the depressing winters. I'd had my share of scares, like when I almost lost the boat over a weir, drowned it in a lock, or the engine broke down in the middle of a river. And most frightening of all, there was the time Cookie had fallen in the canal and been lost all night, with me only being able to rescue her when it got light. Cookie has always been very, very important to me, even more so than my boat.

But I'm getting ahead of myself here. Let's start at the beginning...

Chapter 1
How the Adventure Began

I first started getting interested in boats when I was about 12 years old. My parents had taken me on a day trip to Braunston, near Daventry in Northamptonshire. It was a big canal stop, and there I saw all the gaily painted narrowboats and the people living on them; there was still commercial carrying in those days, so there was a lot to see. I was completely fascinated, so much so that later on at school, when we had to do a lecture in front of the class, I did mine on life on the canals. I researched it by riding down to the local library on my bicycle and borrowing books, reading all I could about boating. My talk included charts and pictures and that sort of thing - and I got a top grade for it. This was most unusual for me as I never normally did well at school.

After that I carried on reading about boating, and one day I borrowed a book called *Narrowboat* by a chap called LTC (Tom) Rolt. It made such an impression on me that I still remember the name nearly half a century later. This book was about a guy who had lived on a narrowboat with his wife through almost all of the 1940s, amongst the traditional narrowboating people. As I read it, something clicked, a germ of an idea, as it were. I suddenly realised it was possible to live for a long time in that way. And I thought, "Wow! I want to do this".

Of course I couldn't; I was too young at the time. And later on I never did. I got a job with British Telecom, discovered girls; then came marriage, responsibility, and living in a house like everyone else. Then I got divorced; and later I remarried and had children and had to earn a living. So everything got in the way of my dream, as tends to happen in life. But the dream never went away, and I still hoped that someday, somehow...

Then in 2004 just about everything changed. My second marriage came to an end, The separation was Jane's idea; she came to me one day and said she'd met someone else. I was pretty devastated, although to be honest we hadn't been getting on well for quite some time. But after the sudden brief thought that I was free, the realisation set in that this was going to be a mess. We ran a business together, a children's nursery. We'd been doing this since 1990, and in 1992 I'd given up my job in BT to do it full time. What was going to happen to it, and what was going to happen to the children, Elizabeth and Joshua, if we couldn't pay the mortgage and had no place to live? It was going to be an absolute nightmare to sort out.

So I decided to run away! We had a holiday flat in Spain, and I went out there in October 2004, a month after Jane had told me she wanted a separation. It was the half term week, and I took a car full of my belongings and drove, along with 16 year old Josh, to Spain, with no intention of ever coming back to the UK. Josh was coming back of course; I'd got him booked on a flight the following week so that he could go back to school. But I was going to stay; I thought I could run the business from a distance. Lizzie was 18, and coming up to 'A' levels, so she really couldn't take any time off at that point.

I lived in Spain for about six months. But around Easter time in 2005 I realised I had to go home, because the business was falling apart, because I missed Lizzie and Josh, and because living in a foreign country is great for a holiday but really hard full time. I had thought I could run the business from afar over the internet; but it turned out that I couldn't. I came back to soaring debts and the problem of selling the business or putting it back on its feet again. I decided I'd have to make it work, because I needed it to pay the mortgage, and I wanted Josh to do his exams without having to move house in the middle. It took me the best part of a year to raise the finance. We had to re-mortgage the nursery building; then pay off the overdraft, the credit card debts, and so on. We finally got it back on a financially viable footing again, and carried on as before. Living separately in the same house wasn't ideal, but the children came first.

However, there were more setbacks to come. In March 2006, my much-loved dad died. He had been ill on and off since having a stroke in 2004, and had actually been admitted to hospital for the first time while I was living in Spain. The initial prognosis had been good and he was expected to recover; however, things didn't work out that way, and after several hospital readmissions, he eventually lost the battle. At least I was able to visit him in hospital and to attend his funeral, but I mourned him terribly.

There was one bright light in the darkness that seemed to envelope my life around that time – and which is extremely relevant to this story. I adopted the eponymous Cookie. She had originally been rescued by my sister Diane, since a friend of Diane's was emigrating to America and needed a home for her cat. My sister, being a kindly sort of person, agreed to adopt the then three year old Cookie. Well...Diane was expecting an ordinary cat, maybe a black and white one, or a tabby, and she was astonished at finding that she had offered a home to a gorgeous, white, long-haired prima donna with a loud miaow and an unpredictable temper! But good as her word she took the kitty home. Cookie coped very well with being a north London cat. She sat in the front window of the house and watched the people go by. She just knew how attractive she looked....and made the most of it (and she still does). There were only two problems. Firstly Diane likes to wear black clothes and Cookie would moult a lot of white fur; and secondly Cookie needs constant grooming and Diane simply didn't have the time. Whenever I went down to visit Diane, Cookie would sit on my knee and I'd comb her, getting out as many knots and mats as I could. Then the next time I'd do it again, though Cookie hardly got groomed at all between my visits.

Well, shortly after dad died, Diane asked me if I wanted Cookie for myself. I adored her and she seemed to like me, so it was a done deal. I took her back to my room at the top of the family house in Tamworth. I don't think she ever left that room because there were other cats in the house and Cookie didn't like other cats. But she seemed very happy, and she quite obviously loved me, sleeping on my bed and watching me as I worked at the little desk I had there.

However, troubles come in threes and there

was more to come. The summer after my dad's death I was back in Spain temporarily for a holiday with Josh. We'd been out for the evening and had a few drinks. Unsurprisingly I got up in the night to go to the loo, and I stood there and....nothing happened. I thought to myself: "Where did all the beer go?" Now I'm pretty aware of men's health issues so I knew that this was not a good thing. I had a routine appointment to see the doctor in England the following week, so I mentioned this to him. He decided to do a blood test, and I booked an appointment for the next week to get the results. It was not good, to say the least. The test used for the presence of cancer in the prostate measures something called Prostate Specific Antigen or PSA. A normal reading is 0 - 3.5. A small operable cancer might come in at 8. Anything over 10 is very serious and, according to the NHS website a reading above 35 means that you are not long for this world. On this scale of 0 – 35, I scored 165. A week later at the hospital it was 204.

The hospital staff tried to be positive, as is their job of course, and I was put on hormone therapy. My PSA then actually came down to about 6. But it looked as though the cancer had spread to the bones, it was too late for an operation or radiotherapy or any of the other usual treatments, and even the Macmillan nurses' leaflets could only offer palliative care. In fact, everyone more or less wrote me off; I was told I had at most about 18 months to live. As I'm sure you can imagine, I went numb with shock. This couldn't be happening to me; this sort of thing only happened to other people. What now?

To start with I didn't tell any of the family that I'd more or less been told I was dying However, Jane guessed that there was something wrong with me, because I had a lot of time off work to go to the hospital. So I had to tell her, and then I told the children. I told Lizzie first but I couldn't have Josh finding out from his sister, so I picked him up from school and told him on the way home. I remember that he just said that it wasn't his best day ever; he'd had a pretty rough day anyway, and he didn't need that! It was a horrible thing to have to tell your teenage children, but they had to know, since I didn't expect to be around for much longer at that point.

Now, the whole family knew that I'd always wanted to live on a boat. Amazingly, they all told me I should go and do it now, while I still could. I still wanted to, but realistically, how could I manage it? By this time I had an additional complication in that I was a cat owner – and there was no way I was going anywhere without Cookie. Lots of people cruise the canals with dogs; I'd never heard of it being done with a cat. Maybe, just maybe, it would be possible; I could try it. But I didn't have any money; we were still barely out of our previous crippling debt. Still, the family was adamant that I should fulfil my long-held dream and go and live on a boat. My sister Diane got involved too at this point. She reminded me that after dad died there had been some money left which was available for the family. It officially belonged to my mum, but she stepped in and told me that I should use it to buy a boat.

So how was I going to pay for food and other necessities? At first I thought I'd take money out of the business to enable me to live on the boat. But I had paid into a pension with BT for many years and I had heard of schemes with insurance companies that could release this money. I had no idea how these work, so I phoned the BT pension people, said I wasn't going to live for long, and asked if any of these schemes are actually possible. The very helpful chap in the call centre said that if I was terminally ill, I could ask for my pension to be paid. I hadn't thought of that, but he told me to write a letter explaining my circumstances, which I did. They then wrote to my GP, and he called me in to talk about how to respond to it; so we actually replied to BT between us. The next thing I knew I got a letter from the pensions people asking for my banking details. I had my pension! I was amazed, for I never expected to have that happen. It seemed as though everything was falling into place.

At this point I should mention that in spite of my almost livelong interest in canals and narrowboats, I'd done very little actual boating. In fact, I'd only tried it once before, for a week. I'd gone on holiday with my family on Jane's brother's timeshare boat; we took my niece and nephew and Lizzie and Josh. We planned a nice easy trip on the canal suitable for young children. But at the last minute the departure point was changed to Evesham on the river Avon, and boating on a river is a totally different ballgame. I had a 60 foot boat, four children, and a wife who wasn't happy with boating. In fact, Jane hadn't really wanted to come, but it was free so she'd decided to give it a go. We took all week to get from Evesham to Stratford and back. In Stratford Jane sought solace in a pub for a while and it took some persuading to get her to come out. The locks on the Avon are monstrous and take a huge amount of skill and experience, which we didn't have. We'd only been shown how to steer the boat, nothing else. So we got to the first lock and the children all ran off with the windlasses and started winding, before we even got the boat in the lock. My mantra became, "Don't run – walk!" On the Avon the water comes in superfast, the locks are wide, and the boat gets buffeted about, so you have to be really careful. The first day we bashed the boat hard enough to break a glass and some crockery , and by the time we got to the last lock of the day it had all become a nightmare. Not only that, but being a river, the banks are owned by the landowners, who have invested in very large 'No Mooring' signs. As a result of this there is hardly anywhere to stop except at the locks. This is frowned on, but we had no choice. So this nice gentle cruise turned into an extremely stressful experience and a bit of a disaster. And, although I'd read a lot over the years, that was all the boating I'd actually done.

Back to October 2006.....I now began to look seriously at boats with a view to buying one. This took quite a while, as none seemed quite right. I started off looking at traditional boats, which have a cabin, an engine in an engine room, and then living space, all on the same level. I looked at several of these, but I decided that although I liked diesel engines very much I didn't want to sleep with one! They were all beautifully polished machines, but I just didn't want to live with the smell of diesel from an engine in the next room. So I switched to looking at the cruiser type boats where the engine is out the back and beneath the deck.

Browsing the internet one day, I saw a boat called *LadyRiverMouse*. I thought to myself, "That's a neat name." And somebody had written underneath, "This is an anagram of 'Live Your Dreams'." Wow! Not only was I seeking to live my dream but I am an avid cryptic crossword fan and the anagram seemed doubly appropriate somehow. The boat was at Crick, in Northamptonshire, and I made an appointment to see it. I even asked mum to come with me, as I was quite sure I'd finally found the boat I wanted.

LadyRiverMouse did indeed seem to tick all the boxes – a shower, good size water, diesel and effluent tanks (essential for living aboard), a nice solid fuel stove but backed up with central heating, and plenty of room in the cabin. Also the engine was out the back below deck - so no living with an engine. I thought that this was it, my search was over. But then I looked in the engine room and my heart sank. It was half full of water, which by any standard is not a good sign! However, the good people at Crick Boat Sales said they'd get it pumped out and cleaned up for us. It turned out to be rain water; the air vents for the engine room were directly under the rainwater run off from the roof. Later on I had the air vents moved, but during my early boating any time after rain I could be seen mopping water from the engine room bilge.

You don't buy a boat without a survey, any more than you would a house. Everything had taken longer than I'd anticipated, and by now it was the end of February 2007. So I phoned the surveyor whom I had been recommended to use. To my surprise he said he could do it really quickly – and then added "in about six weeks". It was my first introduction to narrowboat time; everything works to a slower pace on the waterways. I decided I didn't want to go cruising in the winter anyway and made the appointment.

On the appointed day I drove to Crick, and the boat was already in dry dock. The surveyor was there with a big hammer, looking like he was trying to make holes in *LadyRiverMouse*. I asked him what it was looking like, and he said it seemed pretty good for a 20 year old boat. He then tested the gas, water, electricity, central heating, engine, gearbox, the works. Everything worked. There was a little work which needed to be done to the propeller shaft and a bit of the hull in the engine room was getting thin, but nothing too serious. The boat was advertised for £30,000, but we negotiated for the work that needed doing and paid about £26,000. Mum arranged the payment and at last, in May 2007, accompanied by Josh, I took as many of my belongings as would fit in the car and we drove down to Crick. Josh had decided to come on this first trip, and as many others as he could manage. He wanted to spend time with his dad, while he still could. I was quietly excited. My adventure was about to begin...

LadyRiverMouse

Chapter 2
My First Boating Trip

Josh and I set off in the evening from Crick, somewhat hesitantly, since it was all so new for us. I had only had time to just dump my possessions in the cabin, and, looking back, we had no real idea of what we were doing. But I did realise how inexperienced I was. In fact, this was to be my 'shakedown trip' – a chance to get used to boating, to make sure I actually liked it as much as I expected to, and to gain some experience before I set off alone.

We started off by going along the Leicester arm of the Grand Union Canal, towards Watford and Braunston. The plan was to take *LadyRiverMouse* home to Tamworth for me to pick up the rest of my stuff - and of course my beloved Cookie. She had been left behind in the house for this initial trip, with the family taking care of her. I thought that having her with me was too much to start with; I knew I'd have a very steep learning curve, and I didn't know how Cookie would cope on a boat. I was taking it one step at a time, or trying to. But I had always planned to take her with me. There was no question about it; I wasn't going anywhere without my Cookie!

We could have done with a day or two of easy boating to get used to things, but it didn't work out like that. Right at the start, I had to reverse out of

Crick marina, which was definitely not easy. Then, in quick succession, came Crick tunnel, followed by a complicated set of locks. Nothing like a challenge for two beginners.

Josh and I successfully navigated through Crick tunnel, with its more than a mile of damp, dark, stygian gloominess. Then we came to the top of Watford staircase locks. A 'staircase' of locks is literally that, the top of one lock is the bottom of another, they share gates, and you have to keep going through them in turn. In this case they were padlocked, as we knew they would be, as we were outside the lock-keeper's working hours. So we stopped there by the sanitary station for our first night. It's quite a pretty location so long as you look in the right direction...for behind the mooring thunders six lanes of M1 motorway. The noise was constant, we couldn't get a TV signal, and we hadn't got a radio. Then I tried to fill the water tank and found I had the wrong attachment for the tap. It wasn't the best beginning and I obviously had a great deal to learn, but I was happy and contented as we went to bed, setting the alarm for the lock-keeper's arrival time in the morning.

Lock keepers are a punctual lot and this one was no exception. Even this early in the morning there was a queue of boats waiting. Staircase locks are actually about the most complicated thing a boater meets on the canals. This staircase had five locks, and we knew we had to go through all of them, one after another, without stopping - no mean feat for beginners like us. We were going to go down, and the first boat came up, crewed by a group of young girls from the USA. The lock-keeper was obviously very attracted to these young girls, and he started chatting to them as we started our descent. The first lock went well; then we went into the second one and started to operate it. All of a sudden there was this enormous shout from behind, from the lock-keeper. We'd opened the paddles and let the water in, but we hadn't shut the gates at the other end. We were actually trying to empty the lock above into the valley. In effect we were trying to flood a good portion of Northamptonshire. It was quite serious, or could have been, and we realised that we had made a fundamental error. The lock-keeper yelled at us a bit, and who could blame him. But he was actually there to prevent such a thing happening, and I told him that if he hadn't been so interested in the 'scenery' then he'd have seen us earlier. He got my point, and he helped us from then on. I chalked it all up to experience.

We stopped that night in Braunston. It was actually a tiny distance, but all we felt we could manage at this point. I really wasn't feeling well at all, and I was struggling with any sort of prolonged activity. We arrived at lunchtime and worked the first two locks of the Braunston flight. A flight is a series of locks, but unlike a staircase they are separated by a stretch of water between the two sets of gates, so you don't have to go through them all at once as you do with a staircase. By the side of the canal, in the middle of the flight, was the Admiral Nelson pub. The smell of cooking was drifting over the water, and we decided it was lunchtime. So I tied up the boat, using the equipment which had come with it, which consisted of two iron rods to drive into the bank and a large hammer with which to do so. We had a leisurely lunch in the pub; then returned to discover that our mooring technique had left something to be desired. The stakes had been pulled out of the ground by the wash of a passing boat and *Lady River Mouse* was now floating about in the middle of the canal. Fortunately one end of a rope was still on the bank so we pulled it in – and I realised that I'd have to get better mooring equipment. We decided that was quite enough learning for one day, and that we'd carry on in the morning. After all, I wasn't feeling good and didn't have a lot of stamina; the cancer was clearly taking its toll of my energy.

Next morning at around 9 am I started the engine, and looked at the next lock, which was pretty close. It was going to mean a lot of work, since I was effectively on my own as Josh was still in bed; like many teenagers, it was almost impossible to get him up before midday. Then I had a piece of luck. A singlehanded boater came along, and he asked if I wanted to lash our two boats together side by side, and one of us could steer while the other worked the locks.

So that is what we did. We lashed our boats together in the same way as the working boats used to in past times. I took the first turn at steering, and we'd alternate these tasks. It sounded fine, but the first thing I noticed is that it's almost impossible to steer two boats lashed together using the engine on only one boat. You immediately go round in a circle! But you have to get into a lock only a foot wider than the two boats, so you absolutely have to go straight. Not only that, but the other boat looked like it only came out of a showroom the previous day, and probably cost about a hundred thousand pounds! I was a bit nervous as I really didn't want to scratch what was clearly a very new boat. I could use the rudder, but it was still difficult, and I'd never done anything like this before. I developed instant respect for the old commercial boaters, who must have been incredibly good boat handlers. But somehow I did it. Then we swapped over, and he was a lot better at it than I was, so I worked the paddles and gates until we finally cleared the last lock. Another boating lesson – it is always best to share the work. Then Josh finally surfaced, and off we cruised.

On we went. There were three more locks, and we went through them into a very long 'pound' (the area between locks) between Rugby and Coventry. At Brinklow I contacted my mum as she lived close by, and she and a friend of hers came out to see me. I couldn't get close enough to the bank and they had to use the gangplank, but otherwise their visit went well.

This whole trip was taking much longer than I expected, since it involved some quite complicated boating. I had expected it to take only a few days, but it was clearly going to take much, much longer. I was actually running out of time. Or rather, Josh was; it was his half term, and he had to go back to school as he had exams to take. Boating always takes longer than you think, and I was putting in short days; partly because I wasn't well but also because I had to find out how things worked and find my way around the canal system. So when we got to a convenient spot Josh went back home. Jane came and picked him up, he went back to school, and that left me on my own.

The next day I reached the top of the Atherstone flight of locks. I would have to go through them alone, all eleven of them. I stopped at the top, and I thought I'd do them in the morning. I got up early next day and went into the first lock. I emptied it, as I was going down; then I opened the bottom gate and cruised out to a grinding halt! There was not enough water in the pound between the first and second locks; it had drained out overnight as there was a leak in the pound. You could see water, but it was only six inches deep; it looked OK, but I needed at least 18 inches to float *LadyRiverMouse*. Oh dear! And there was no-one around to help me. Being an engineer I realised that I had to let more water out of the pound at the top, but being a novice when it came to boating I was a bit nervous. So I filled the lock, then emptied it again, rather than just letting in what I needed. In fact I did this a couple of times, determined to get enough water. Of course, later on when I was experienced I would have just opened the paddles and let water in until had what I needed.

So I got through the pound...and there were only another ten locks to do! The first five were fairly close together; then there was a gap. I didn't really know how to handle the boat and operate locks single handedly. When there are two people, you can drop off one, and he or she operates the lock while you manoeuvre the boat. If you're alone, you have to do both jobs. This means a lot of tying up and untying! Also, in wide locks, you need to control the boat with a rope while the lock is filling or emptying, to prevent it buffeting about. It's not easy, and locks are probably about three times as much work for one person as for two.

These were narrow locks, so not really all that difficult, but I was actually having to learn how to do all of this as I went along. There were no disasters until about the sixth lock, when I nearly fell in! I put a foot on the boat from the bank and missed my footing, just managing to grasp a handrail and prevent an unplanned swim. I realised then that I was going to have to be more careful.

Eventually, with much work, I cleared all eleven locks, and by mid-afternoon I tied up for the day. As I sipped my afternoon tea I reflected that operating eleven locks single handedly is not bad for someone who is terminally ill. I didn't realise then, but that was perhaps the first indication that maybe the doctors didn't know everything

Despite the difficulties and the fact that I was feeling ill, it never occurred to me that I'd bitten off more than I could chew with this whole venture. I was having a great time. I loved it! I enjoyed the way it was so quiet and peaceful. Every morning I opened the side window and there was rippling water with an abundance of wildlife and tranquillity. Despite the difficulties, I just loved everything about boating already...floating through the countryside at four miles an hour while everyone else was buzzing along at about 70mph. This was the life for me and it got under my skin.

When I got to Polesworth I had to go to the shop as I'd run out of food. I moored at the visitor moorings and went up into the town, and I couldn't understand why the traffic was going so fast. How come they'd all speeded up, in only a few days? That's how it felt to me, and that feeling never left me throughout my time on the boat: the world is living far too quickly, slow down a bit.

It took me about two weeks to get the boat back to Tamworth. This wasn't the best boating time in the world, but I was really in no hurry. I thought I'd already learned quite a lot, but I found out later that I still had a great deal to learn. Still, I was acquiring knowledge all the time.

It took me about three weeks to move my belongings the quarter mile from our old house to the canal where I had moored *LadyRiverMouse.* Almost the very last thing I did was move Cookie on board, along with her food bowls, litter tray, and other cat paraphernalia. Just before I was about to leave, something happened which made me realise that I would have to be very careful of my cat. I was loading some final items aboard, and Cookie, taking a stroll round the deck, missed her footing and fell from the boat into the canal. It was very scary, as she fell between the boat and the bank. Because of the way the bank was shaped, there was enough room for her down there in the water, but I couldn't get her back up through the gap. I had to grab hold of her by the scruff of her neck and tow her along in the water until there was more room between the boat and the bank. I thought that would be a lesson well learnt and she'd never do such a thing again – but she did. She didn't seem to realise that the water was dangerous, though that's another story...

Despite this incident, I wasn't really all that worried about how I'd manage on a boat with a cat in the long term. In fact, few cats live on boats, dogs being the normal pet of choice for boaters; but I thought I'd work out how to manage as I went along. Cookie had always been an indoor cat so being confined for long periods in the cabin was not a problem; I'd just have to watch her carefully when she ventured outside.

It was late May 2007, and I was now ready to begin my new life in earnest.

Chapter 3
First Solo Cruise

I was ready to go on my first real cruise! The decision on where to go was quite simple. I wanted an easy trip for my first one on my own with Cookie, and that meant the Ashby canal   The Ashby has several advantages. It's a lovely route through glorious countryside, it's quiet with little boat traffic as it doesn't form a through route, and in all its 22 miles there is not a single lock.

However, to get to the Ashby I had to go back through Atherstone with its flight of eleven locks. They were still a daunting prospect for me, though during my boating years I went up and down those locks so many times that we eventually became old friends. But that was not the case at this point. All the same, it was easier this time than it had been the first time as I was more used to it. Also, I stopped halfway at a boatyard to pick up some diesel, so that gave me a break and made the trip slightly more restful.

The Ashby looked all very nice and peaceful and I was already becoming used to this boating lark. I did have one big reservation, however. At the very start of the Ashby, it becomes extremely narrow. This is a common feature on canals and is left over from the times when the original canal companies guarded their water supplies with gates at the entrance to their route. It also helped when collecting the all-important tolls. But earlier on I'd met somebody who had been living on board his boat with two cats, and at this point his cats had jumped ship and he'd never seen them again. So I was very, very careful of my Cookie as we drifted though the narrow gap.

Cookie got used to boating surprisingly quickly, and she did very well during this early period. She would come and sit on the back step and just watch the scenery go by. She usually didn't try to escape or to go anywhere, but then, she'd never been that sort of cat. She seemed very contented. She had me, and she had a home even if it moved, and that seemed to be fine with her. She just lived a normal cat's life – eating, sleeping, asking to be stroked. Sometimes at this stage she would go out for a little wander along the bank, and then she'd come back.

However, at the top of the Atherstone locks I had a bit of a shock when I lost her temporarily over the backs of the houses. I had moored up at the top of the locks, and she went ashore, as she liked to do. But this time she jumped over the fence of a garden that backed on to the canal, and then she disappeared up the garden path towards the house. I was watching her, but I couldn't get over the fence. She then went from that house to the next house. She looked through their French windows and went "Miaow" and then went on to the next house, and there I was, on the towpath, wondering how I was going to get my cat back.

At that point someone came into one of the gardens, and I shouted from the towpath, "Excuse me, can I have my cat back please". The person looked at me a little strangely. Then Cookie took one look at this person and clearly decided that she didn't like him. She came running up the garden - but it wasn't the fence that she'd jumped over to get into the gardens originally; this one was much taller. I could see the problem she was going to have; she wasn't going to be able to get over. But cats are cats, even non-athletic fluffy white Cookie cats. She took a flying leap off the top of a compost heap, cleared the fence, and landed back by the boat. So ended one of her early little forays into the outside world. As I watched her, I reminded myself again that I was going to have to be very careful with my cat. From then on I started looking for 'Cookie-safe' moorings, ie moorings with fences that she couldn't get through, or over. She wasn't really the most agile of cats, and if there was a good chain link fence then she couldn't get through it. This was the start of my realisation that I'd have to fit in the type of boating I did with the way Cookie was. But that was OK; Cookie always came first with me.

So I trugged on up the Ashby canal. Something I found out and made a note of for the future - if you visit the Ashby you need to take a lot of provisions with you. The nearest place you can get to a shop is Market Bosworth and it's a good mile uphill from any mooring. But there are places to visit, and the boating was easy until we got right to the end; a place called Moira. There was a short tunnel before reaching Moira, and we went though it to a little basin where you could tie up. As I moored I thought that it might be a nice place to stay for a little while. However, just as I started tying the mooring ropes, three huge German Shepherd dogs bounded off the boat in front. Cookie didn't like dogs and was not going to appreciate being next door to these three. Best to just turn round and set off back...

Things went pretty well on this shakedown cruise and I started to sort out where everything should go on the boat. This took a little while, because I didn't have a great deal of space, especially for a cat and all her paraphernalia. But I found that Cookie's litter tray would go under the back step, and I managed to provide her with her own little place for her food dishes and her scratching post and all the rest of the things a cat demands. On her side, she started to sleep on my chair next to the bed, and to really make herself at home. We were both settling in and learning the boating way of life.

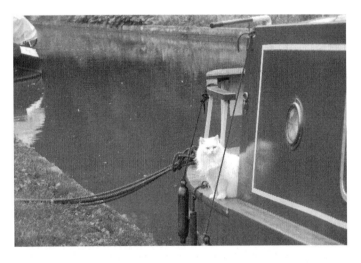

Cookie checking out a new mooring. "Are there any dogs?"

Chapter 4
The East Midlands Ring

After this first little trip I went back to Tamworth...and decided that I now wanted a longer, more demanding, cruise. I wanted to find out what my boat would do, and I decided to take her on a river. The nearest river was the Trent, so I planned to do the East Midlands Ring, as it was known. That meant boating from Tamworth to Fradley Junction, then Burton-on-Trent, then Shardlow, on to the great wide Trent, from which the River Soar leads to Loughborough, Leicester, and then back down to Crick - and the last little bit from Crick to Tamworth I'd already done when I brought *LadyRiverMouse* back. So once I got to Crick I would have effectively completed the ring.

I set off one sunny afternoon in the direction of Fradley. It was now June, so getting warmer, with long days. Early on I got in a bit of a tangle in Alrewas lock because I forgot to close the top paddles while emptying the lock. *LadyRiverMouse* was swept back by the swirling water and hit the top gate with a mighty clang. A beginner's mistake and a very common one, but even though I hadn't been boating for long, I felt I should be better than this by now. I didn't seem to have caused any damage, so I carried on a little bit further. Then all at once I seemed to be sailing though a sea of diesel. My first thought was that I had ruptured the diesel tank which was exactly where the collision had occurred. There was not much choice but to carry on to the next marina – fortunately not far – but as I boated on the sea of oil abated. Panic over; it was a false alarm, a spill from another boat. Phew! Time for a cup of tea and a stroke of Cookie.

I boated through Burton-on-Trent, and in due course came to Stenson lock which is big and wide, and scary. I wasn't looking forward to this on my own, and to add to my troubles, just as I was approaching the alternator failed. Not good - without the alternator I had no way of charging the batteries essential for life on board in many ways – not least of which was to start the engine of course! It had been playing up for a little while, in the way that mechanical things sometimes do, and I'd already taken it to a boatyard on the Ashby canal to get it checked over. They'd looked at it and said that they'd seen worse and it would be alright. That wasn't to be the last time I was to receive rather over-optimistic advice from a boatyard. I tied up by the little boatyard above Stenson lock and went into their office, with my tale of woe, and asked if they could do anything. They said that they were very busy, but if I could get the broken part off the boat myself then they would take it into Derby that afternoon and would get a new one; plus they would only charge me the cost price. That sounded good to me so I went back to *LadyRiverMouse* and broke out the spanners.

It only took me a few minutes to remove, and soon I was back in the office with the offending part. They were as good as their word, and by about 5 o'clock I'd got a new alternator, which I put on the boat. Alternators do die of old age but this one had suffered from a different problem; it was full of oil. I did a little bit of investigation and discovered that the oil was coming from the crankcase breather on top of the engine. It wasn't really a fault, but the engine was old and wheezing oil all over the place; and this oil was flying across to the alternator, getting into it, and stopping it working. A bit of thinking, and I came up with a plan to stop that happening. It took me a while, but I fitted a hose to the crankcase breather and fed the fumes back into the engine inlet so that it burned the oil and it didn't all go into the alternator. I was very proud of that. It occurred to me then for the first time that there were many things you needed to know if you were going to live on a boat, particularly if it was a very old boat like *LadyRiverMouse*. You need a good knowledge of diesel engines, and you need a very good understanding of lead acid batteries. If you don't start off with that knowledge, you're going to get it as time goes by, whether you like it or not. However, despite the apparent snags, boating was turning out to be all I'd hoped it would be; it was a wonderful way of life. I was enjoying it more and more.

Stenson is the first of the locks on the lower Trent and Mersey canal, which are all wide, deep and scary. In these circumstances it pays to share if you can, and I teamed up with a couple from Sheffield on their way back to their home mooring at Shardlow. Sharing locks, ie going though together, cuts the work down by about two-thirds – there's half as much leaping on and off the boat to operate the locks. Also, two boats in a wide lock fit better, which means you don't have to tie up to stop your boat floating around.

It makes everything so much easier. But then a funny thing happened. On one of the pounds between the locks, I was in front, and I looked back, to see this couple's boat getting closer and closer. I wondered if they thought I was going too slowly, so I speeded up a little. Then they got closer again, so I speeded up some more. We were going pretty fast now, and I thought we'd go waterskiiing in a minute but after a little while they dropped back a bit, and I thought I was finally going fast enough for them. All became clear when we both stopped at the next lock, and the lady of the couple presented me with a photograph that she'd taken of me steering *LadyRiverMouse*. That was why they'd come so close, so that they could get a good picture. They'd taken this photo, printed it on their printer on board, and given it to me. I've never been so touched; in fact I was in tears and I just didn't know what to say. It was perhaps my first example of the sort of kindness you can sometimes find on the waterways.

I left these kind people at Shardlow and I carried on alone, on to the great wide waters of the Trent with Trumpton weir looming to catch the unwary, under the M1 motorway and on to the river Soar. I'd got ideas from reading guidebooks that *LadyRiverMouse* might not have enough engine power to cope with the river; we could be swept over the weir and Cookie and I would drown in the swirling waters. Narrowboats aren't very powerful, and rivers are, and I thought it might be a problem in a boat which was 20 years old. So I decided to go carefully and give the weir a wide berth. But the boat behaved beautifully on the river, and I had no problems. Time and again *LadyRiverMouse* would prove that she was up to all that I asked of her. A turn off the Trent leads to the tributary river, the Soar. Here I met a 'trip boat' and shared locks with them. This boat was full of pensioners out on a day trip with a professional crew who worked the locks with ease, so all I had to do was stay close.

All came to a halt at Loughborough – the lock there had suffered some damage, reportedly from a passing hire boat. It's odd how hire boats always get the blame for these things – privately owned boats never damage locks of course... There was a short delay while British Waterways sent a crane to lift the lock gate back on to its hinges, but by then it was too late to go on further. So I tied up in Loughborough town centre.

Now, a slight but relevant digression... Before I set out from Tamworth on this particular trip, I had met Gerald. Gerald was in his 70s, and living alone on his narrowboat; he had done so for years. He knew just about everything there was to know about boating, and he invited me on board for a cup of tea. I remember that I was a little bit alarmed because he had a generator running in his living space, with the exhaust pipe pointing out of the window, which breaks just about every rule in the book, and is extremely dangerous by any standards. But Gerald had been doing it for years and there was no stopping him now. In spite of my concerns at the danger, we shared tea and cake before going our separate ways.

Back in Loughborough I tied up for the night. But then I woke up and I could tell that things weren't right. I got out of bed and the boat moved! Normally you tie up to the bank, which steadies the boat and it doesn't move. I looked out of the window, and where there should be bank there was water. I'd been cast adrift, and I was floating down the river Soar towards a weir. This, needless to say, is not a good thing. I quickly got some clothes on, climbed out on deck and got the engine started. In getting back to a mooring I did rather demolish an already very dilapidated landing stage. If this was at all valuable I apologise now, but I was escaping from a desperate situation.

Following this incident I decided that when moored in a town it would be better to chain the boat up with a locking device, so a lesson was learned. I also thought I ought to tell someone that this was happening. So as I was leaving in the morning I said to the person in the boat next to me, "Be careful, I got cast adrift here last night". Then I carried on along the gloriously clear waters of the Soar towards Kegworth, where I tied up that evening. Lo and behold - there was Gerald again. We were both going round the ring in opposite directions, and we'd met halfway. I said hello, and added, "You'll never guess what happened to me, I got cast adrift last night". And he looked at me and he said, "Oh, it was you!" Word of my getting cast adrift had reached Kegworth faster than I had. That was the first time I came upon something called the 'towpath telegraph' - a gossip system by means of which news travels like lightening up and down the canal system.

So I carried on along the river. Now, rivers go into flood occasionally. You know when they do that because there are depth gauges at the locks. If the gauge is 'in the red' you don't go. At least, that is supposed to be the case. I was sailing south towards Leicester, and the depth gauges were showing green and all was well. But then I arrived at a section of river where there were a lot of lakes that weren't on my map. I carried on boating through them anyway. The gauge by the next lock revealed why the extra lakes were there. The section of river I was boating in was well into the red. There hadn't been a marker at the beginning – or maybe it was underwater - so I'd carried on regardless. I shouldn't have been there but as it happened I didn't have any trouble; the water level was dropping quite quickly. At the point where you tie up before the lock, the landing stage was under water, and I had to wait a minute or two for the water level to go down. As I worked though the lock I reflected that I had sailed though a river on 'red boards' without any difficulty at all, and I thought that I must be really getting the hang of this boating lark.

Leicester should have been my next port of call. It is described as one of the most beautiful entrances into a city by canal that you can possibly get. But it's also known for crime and vandalism, which means there are miles of beautiful moorings with not a boat on any of them. There's a secure mooring behind a fence, with a gate protected by lock and key, but that little area was crowded with boats. There was no room there for *LadyRiverMouse,* so I just sailed straight through the town. But I'd worked in Leicester for a few years and I knew the place well, so I didn't really need to visit. I just stopped briefly for lunch, then I carried on a few miles to the suburb of Aylestone.

You might wonder how I planned each day. Actually I didn't, not really. I had no real routine; that was the joy of boating. I just did what suited me. I didn't have any set hours; I got up and sailed until I found a nice spot, and then I stopped. The amount of time I sailed varied a lot – it could be two hours, four hours, it might be only half an hour. I wasn't doing full days though; I didn't want to, and wasn't feeling well enough to even if I did.

In Aylestone I bought a folding bike. I decided that walking miles to shops really was getting me down, and shopping could be better done with a bicycle. Every time I stopped I needed to pick up provisions, and some times were more difficult than others, the biggest problem being fresh fruit and vegetables. I couldn't find them anywhere near the canal in Burton-on-Trent, or in Shardlow. I had gone for almost two weeks living out of tins because that was all I could find to buy. With a bike I could go a bit further to get to shops, maybe even to a supermarket. This wasn't a worry to Cookie of course; I took plenty of cat food with me, but you can always buy it in just about every corner shop. Cat litter I never actually ran out of, but sometimes poor Cookie had to manage a bit longer with her tray than would have been ideal.

Talking of Cookie, it was in the Leicester area that I decided that Cookie really couldn't be allowed out on deck when the boat was in locks. I had let *LadyRiverMouse* down in a lock, and was about to climb down the ladder. Looking down there was Cookie taking a stroll on deck just a short distance from the whirlpools that form in a lock as the water enters. I decided that was far too dangerous. So I introduced a new routine at locks - Cookie would go down below in the cabin, and I'd shut the doors to keep her in. I was learning that I had to make a few adjustments to keep her safe, but on the whole, Cookie adapted really well to this boating life. Once she got the idea that *LadyRiverMouse* was home she was fine, even if it did move now and again. The big noisy diesel engine that I had nicknamed Bertha rumbling away in the background wasn't going to eat her – though I think she was never quite sure on this last point.

The locks south of Leicester have been described as completely devoid of interest and it rained incessantly the whole weekend I was there. A little boatyard at Kilby Bridge offered the last chance for a while to fill up my domestic water tank and empty the effluent and while I was doing this Cookie took a little stroll around. When my tanks were sorted Cookie was nowhere to be found. I called her, but cats are not dogs when it comes to answering to their name. Then it came to me – think like a cat; it's raining; where is there shelter? It took only a minute to find the white fluffball hiding under a pallet of stuff not far from where I had been working. Getting her out took a while longer and a good offering of favourite cat treats.

I didn't meet another soul the whole wet weekend that I worked the locks south of Leicester. At one point it rained so hard that I left *LadyRiverMouse* drifting in a lock while I took cover from the deluge. It was really hard boating, but then I went through a short tunnel and out into a completely different world. This was the canal mecca called Foxton. Here there were staircase locks, a museum, an incline plane and all sorts of canal memorabilia. Boats and people were everywhere. The sun came out and the world filled with colour. I made sure Cookie was down below; I didn't want her running off in all these crowds. Then I went into the canal shop and bought myself some serious lock operating kit - lightweight alloy windlasses. The ones that had come with *LadyRiverMouse* were serviceable but I had struggled with their weight, and lightweight kit would make all the difference in future.

From here there was a little canal arm that wended its way to the town of Market Harborough. I needed provisions, so I decided to go there. On the way was a swing bridge, my first one. The problem with swing bridges when you're single handed is that you have to tie the boat up to the towpath, go over the bridge, open the bridge - but then you can't get back over the bridge to get back to the boat. Every bridge is different but here a little sign on the towpath told boaters that the trick was to moor the boat diagonally across the canal, so that you could get on and off from the 'wrong' side. You can't always do it with all swing bridges; sometimes the canal is too wide. Each one you have to work out separately so it was nice to have a clue in this case. So I wedged *LadyRiverMouse* across the canal, and as I went to close the road barriers prior to opening the bridge, a car came along. I wondered whether to let him through, but if I kept doing that, I could be there all day. So I carried on, opened the bridge, climbed back on to my boat, went through the bridge, moored up diagonally again, and closed the bridge. Then, as I was leaving, the car window wound down. I was ready for an earful of abuse but what he actually said was "I've lived here 20 years and been coming across this bridge all that time. That's the first time I've ever seen anybody do it on their own; I wondered how it was done". I was really quite proud of myself.

Cookie and I were now developing a bit of a routine. She would wander off at times, and I remember phoning my sister in a panic once and saying, "Does Cookie stay out very long?" Then she came back of course. The saving grace was that she didn't like dogs, and the towpaths were full of dogs and dog walkers. I would tie up, and she would come up on deck, take a sniff at the towpath, decide there were dogs there, and go back down again. This suited me just fine. One of the problems I had was that when she did go ashore she couldn't always work out which boat she had to come back to. She knew she lived on a boat, but she wasn't quite sure which one of them it was. On some occasions I'd find her sitting on some very posh boat clearly saying, "Can we have this one please".

There were shops in Market Harborough, thank goodness, and I managed to fill up my cupboards again. I was now realising that you have to carry a lot of stuff with you that lasts a long time. I would have to live out of tins and packets a lot, because I didn't have the battery capacity to run a freezer. A word here on how that worked.... Lead acid batteries are relatively cheap, and potentially provide lots of power. But but they have one big problem; they take 30 hours to fully recharge. Even running the engine for five or six hours a day will not recharge them fully. There are all sorts of systems devised for rapid charging of batteries, but if you use those then you will shorten the life of the battery. This is just a problem with lead acid technology, Things may have moved on now; I don't know - you may be able to use lithium ions or similar batteries. But lead acid is cheap and rugged technology, so I suspect that it has a long life yet in the world of narrowboating, and boaters will be living with its shortcomings for a while yet. This was summer, so lighting wasn't a problem, but fridges use more power than you think and storing food safely was a priority. I suppose I could have gone out for meals, at least in some places, and later on when Josh was with me we did; but I don't like doing that alone.

My next job was working the Foxton locks, two staircases, one after the other. As you will remember from my experience at Watford with staircases, once you've started, you can't stop. The lock keepers direct the boats through in groups, about five at a time. I was scheduled in the middle of one of these groups, and I told the lock keeper that I was on my own, so I might be slow and hold things up. He said there was no problem; it would be alright and there was no rush, but I was still concerned about holding things up as there was quite a queue of boats waiting. To begin with my fears were realised; as I got through the first two locks the boats in front of me were disappearing into the distance. But at this point help arrived from an unexpected quarter. A school party turned up on the bank. Calls erupted across the water: "Can we open the gates", and "Can we wind the paddles". I told them what to do, and they were brilliant. I think they were from an inner city school and had never seen canals before. They were thrilled to help, and I was just as thrilled to have them. I don't know what their teacher thought about health and safety and so on, but they didn't run, and they did as they were told. I was soon catching the other boats up.

At the top I tied up and had a look round and a bite to eat in the cafe. Then, as I was getting back aboard *LadyRiverMouse*, a complete stranger approached carrying a bag. He said, "I thought you might like some plums; we've got so many on our tree we don't know what to do with them". I love plums; they're my favourite fruit and these were lovely. I thought that this boating was marvellous; people help you out and come up and give you things. What a wonderful way of life.

In Husbands Bosworth I saw a shop on my map, moored and climbed up the bank. I hadn't walked more than a few paces before a car stopped and I was offered a lift into the village. There I found a small shop, packed with 'free from' food. It turned out that there was a young girl in the village with coeliac disease and they stocked it for her. For me this was wonderful. I was mostly vegetarian at this point; at least, I was trying to be, but it was very difficult when I had to buy everything from village shops. I was also trying not to eat gluten, as I'd heard that a gluten-free diet could help with cancer. In fact, I was trying all sorts of things diet-wise for this, and I had a cupboard full of complementary medicine type cures too; apricot kernels featured large in this regime but I would try anything and everything. Actually, my health wasn't too bad at this point; I wasn't doing long days, but for someone terminally ill I thought I was doing pretty well. And yet again, I wondered...

Somewhere along the Leicester arm of the Grand Union, I tied up next to a boat which was notable because the owner was keeping chickens on the bank. I thought that was pretty neat, but also that I'd better keep Cookie away from them. An old lady lived on this boat, and I asked her if she was allowed to keep chickens on the towpath, and how long she could stay there. She told me: "I stop here until they stick a notice on my boat, and then I move. And I advise you to do the same". So I filed that away for future reference, and later on I was to take that advice. Life is not made easy for those living on boats permanently. Two weeks is the longest you're allowed to stay anywhere, and many visitor moorings are less than that. Residential moorings are like rocking horse manure; to get one you'll have to get on a waiting list which is probably longer than your remaining lifespan. Most people who live on boats stay in marinas, which is like living in a holiday home, in that they really shouldn't do it. Councils vary, but usually you're allowed six months in a marina. Some marinas have arrangements whereby occupants can swap between two or more marinas every six months. Out on the towpath though, the general rule is 14 days maximum. After that British Waterways can start to issue you with notices telling you to move. Eventually they can take your boat out of the water; it's a long process, but it can and does happen. I knew all this before I started, and I also knew that enforcement of these mooring regulations is extremely patchy. I was to find out much more about mooring wardens later...

I was now in Crick. I'd completed the ring. I'd done Crick to Tamworth before of course and as before I stopped off in the canal mecca that is Braunston. It was the August bank holiday and the place was packed to bursting with people and boats. I found a mooring, but boats continued to arrive, and soon they were moored both sides with just room for a single lane in the middle. I decided that this was not my idea of fun at all, so I rose very early the next morning and crept away before the multitudes woke up. I ended my first summer back in Tamworth. It had gone extremely well and I was very happy with my new lifestyle. Cookie had settled in well and all seemed rosy. But I hadn't lived through a winter yet...

Chapter 5
First Winter Aboard

It was now September, and the last few weeks of the dying cruising season. I did some local boating, cruising up and down between Tamworth and Polesworth and then out towards Fradley and back again, moving backwards and forwards every 14 days. I did that several times. When I was not actually boating I was titivating my boat, as it were; I was painting, and arranging things, and moving stuff. I moved shelves, I redesigned the windows so that they could be lifted out rather than just slid back, I worked on the myriad of jobs that you do when you've just moved into a place, be it on land or on the water. I went to the boat show and bought myself a little TV. And I bought a radio, and this was the start of one of the most frightening events of my whole five years. It concerned Cookie of course...

It was now autumn, but we were having an Indian summer. I went to Halfords to buy a car radio, which with 12 volt electrics sounded like the right thing to have on a boat. I walked in and asked for a radio, and an aerial, and some speakers. The assistant asked all sorts of technical questions but couldn't recommend one with a remote control, which I would have liked. Cars don't need these, apparently. Eventually I ignored all the technical stuff and just chose the one with a red display as it fitted my colour scheme. I remember that I had to go across the road to Argos for the speakers; amazing the things which stick in your mind. I went back to the boat, which was moored in Polesworth, with all my goodies, and I started to install everything. The first thing that fell from the box was a remote control; I had one after all. I had cables to lay, and screws to put in, and holes to make. It was a beautiful sunny day, and so I had all the doors and windows open. I was busy fitting the radio, and having a great time. Then I turned round, and there was no Cookie. She'd gone. I went out looking for her, calling, "Cookie, Cookie, where are you Cookie?" She does sometimes turn up when I call her, but this time she didn't.

I sat up all that night with the doors open, waiting for Cookie to come home, listening to the distant church clock chiming away the hours. At first light, which was about 4 am, with no colour in the world and everything grey, I decided I was going out to look for my Cookie. I had to do something; I was beside myself by now. I got up on to the bank, and called Cookie's name, in as loud a voice as I reasonably could at that hour. After a few calls I thought I heard a faint miaow. I had only one thought: "It must be Cookie!" I called again, and got another miaow. I couldn't work out the direction it was coming from but as I got nearer the water, the miaow was a little louder, and as I moved away it became quieter. Then the world got a little lighter, and I looked up, and there she was on the opposite bank. She was soaking wet, cold, covered in mud and looking very sorry for herself. She'd obviously fallen in the canal, and hadn't been able to get out on the boat side because the bank was a vertical wall, so she'd swum across the canal and climbed out into the trees on the opposite side. She'd clearly been there for a while, poor cat.

Well, I wasn't going to let my Cookie stay stuck over there, even if it was still the middle of the night. So I cast off and started the engine. It wasn't the quietest of engines. It's not illegal to do this at night, but it is somewhat antisocial. I didn't care; I revved the engine, put *LadyRiverMouse* into gear, and went over to the other bank to rescue my Cookie. But it wasn't that easy. I got within three feet of the bank, but I couldn't get any closer as the water was too shallow. So I wrapped a rope around a tree to tether the boat, and jumped the three feet to the shore. Cookie ran up and jumped into my arms. It was lovely to have her back, and I held her and just said over and over again, "Cookie, oh my Cookie". But she was shivering and I knew I had to get her back to the boat. Then I realised I had a problem; there I was, holding a cat, and I had three feet to jump, muddy shoes, and a slippery deck to land on. I needed my arms, but they were full of Cookie. Only one thing for it - I leaned forward as far as I could and as gently as possible tossed Cookie on to the deck. She disappeared down below like muddy white lightning. I got back on the boat, and with more revving of the engine and churning of water, I got back to the mooring and tied up. Then I went down below and got Cookie in some hot water, and cleaned the mud off her and warmed her up. I was really, really pleased to see my cat and she seemed even more pleased to see me. She'd obviously had a rough night, poor Cookie.

This is not quite the end of the story. Later that morning, I apologised to an Australian couple on the boat behind me. I said that I was sorry for waking them up in the early hours of the morning, explaining that my cat had been stuck on the opposite side, and I'd been looking for her for ages. One of them paused. "White cat?", he asked. "Yes", I replied. And they said they'd seen her swimming round in the water the previous afternoon. I was not happy. I'd been calling Cookie, they must have heard me, they knew where she was, and they never said anything. Perhaps unfairly, I went really off Australians for a long time after that.

It was now October, and coming up to winter. Late October is the start of the official closed season for canal boating. The canals close down, and British Waterways use the time for maintenance. This means that large stretches of the waterways are shut, and locks are closed because they need to do maintenance on them; they need to repair the gates, put in ladders, mend all the sort of stuff that we boaters moan about if it's not working in the summer. That all has to be done regularly, and they choose the winter because there aren't so many people wanting to go boating in the winter.

I spent that winter on the Coventry canal between Atherstone and Fradley. I stayed rather a long time in Fazeley, right opposite the British Waterways offices, on a 14 day mooring! I was there for a couple of months, waving at the staff as they went in and out. British Waterways get a little more lax about mooring during the winter. They can't move you on because there's nowhere for you to go as the locks are mostly closed for maintenance. I was to meet a slightly different attitude the following winter, but that year, in the Midlands, they were very relaxed about it. I couldn't get into a marina; I did try, but they didn't have any space. So I just just trugged about a bit, up and down a short stretch of the canal. I spent the whole of December and January, the coldest months of the winter, in the area. There was a sanitary station there, which meant every so often I'd take the boat across the canal and empty the toilet and waste bins and fill up the water tank, and then just move back again. Apart from that I just stayed put. And I wasn't the only person doing that; there were several boats there, at least a dozen in fact. I was still fairly new to boating and not altogether sure about these things, but there is strength in numbers and I wouldn't be the only one in trouble if anyone were to complain about us.

Not everything is always peaceful between neighbours, even on the waterways. Two of the boaters fell out to the point of fisticuffs over the moorings along this stretch of canal. The problem was that there was a very small area where there was no TV reception, and while somebody went across to empty their toilet, another boat moved forward into their spot. They literally came to blows over this.

I also remember a countryside ranger, a lovely chap; he'd come along and sort out disputes sometimes. He took it upon himself to keep that stretch of canal tidy. He wore a uniform of sorts, with pockets and compasses hanging off him, although I don't think he had any official capacity. He became a friend and used to come along and say hello to me and to Cookie, who everyone adored - as is her expectation and right of course!

People outside the boating community were curious when they heard that I lived on a boat. Their most frequent question concerned whether I was cold in the winter. I wasn't cold, so long as I could get enough coal. I had a solid fuel stove, plus gas central heating firing three radiators. The gas heating I only used as a reserve as it was very heavy on gas. It could empty a bottle of calor gas in three days, and I decided that this had to stop. Not only is gas expensive but the bottles are heavy, and manhandling them into their locker right in the bows was a job to be done as rarely as possible. The solid fuel heating was much better; coal was fine if there was enough of it, and I spent the winter carrying bags of coal up and down the towpath from the local supermarket.

So what do boaters do over winter? That was another question I used to get asked. Most of the time we just keep our heads down. I tried to keep on top of the cleaning – especially the outside brasswork which always speaks of a well kept craft if it has a good polish to it. To begin with I had quite a lot of fixing up to do - but by winter I'd really got the boat more or less the way I wanted it. So in the depths of winter I went down below and lit my stove which kept me toasty warm. The internet is a godsend for boaters and I spent a lot of time surfing the web, as I still do. And I stroked my cat a lot. Cookie got used to being in Fazeley and went out quite often. One night she was somewhat late back and I got a bit panicky, but she did come back eventually. That winter was quite mild, and I took fairly regular trips up towards Fradley, because it's quite a nice run, and I needed to charge the batteries regularly. Later on in Fazeley, on that same mooring, boaters incurred the wrath of the local residents, because they were running their engines to charge the batteries. There was violence - car tyres were slashed, boats were attacked, and other things like that. That was after I had left though; there was nothing like that during the time I was there. It was quite a peaceful winter overall.

Everything opens up for Easter, so usually during March things started to get back to normal, and I prepared to leave. I'd made plans for the next summer; I was going to head south, and more specifically I was going to London. I remember saying to my ranger friend, "I'm leaving now, I'll see you in a few months". It turned out to be a couple of years!

So I left, and as I boated through Tamworth I picked up Josh, who had been staying at his mum's house over winter. He was now ready to come with me, and help with the 102 locks on the long trip between Rugby and London! Josh had decided to take a year out before university and to spend the summer boating with me. Because I was so ill, he thought it might be his last chance to spend time with his dad. Of course I was delighted to have him along.

Josh working a narrow lock

Chapter 6
Boating to London

The three of us - me, Josh and Cookie - boated over the stretch I'd already done so many times; south down to Braunston, then on towards Crick. But when we got to Norton Junction, instead of turning left for the Leicester Arm and Crick, which was the route we had covered before, we went straight on south, taking the Grand Union Main Line towards London.

To start with the boating was nice and easy. There were few locks and those there were we managed to share with another boat, which halved the work. It was a good thing that it was easy, because the weather was appalling. The rain positively tipped down. This was March 2008, and all through Easter it poured with rain. Then through the gloom came the dismal outline of the entrance to Blisworth Tunnel. I thought, "Thank goodness for that!" It's not very often that you're grateful for a tunnel, but I thought that at least it wouldn't be raining in there. It was a stupid thought, for Blisworth Tunnel is the wettest in the country; halfway through a stream flows through the roof in a big cascade. Frying pans and fire sprang to mind...

As we came out of Blisworth tunnel, we arrived at the village of Stoke Bruerne, a big and popular canal centre. I stopped, deciding to have a couple of days there to look around. We moored up, and went to the pub for the evening. The couple that we had been sharing locks with were there too and a good night was had by all. It had finally stopped raining, and we went to bed that night hoping that the weather had taken a turn for the better.

We woke up next morning and the whole world was white! There was about two inches of snow on everything - this was Easter 2008. Then the boat's carbon monoxide alarm went off. There were a lot of alarms on *LadyRiverMouse* and they all sounded the same so it me took a moment to work out what it was. When I did, I panicked a bit and opened all doors and windows wide, which must have looked odd to passers by in the snow, but carbon monoxide is extremely dangerous and I wasn't about to take any risks. Eventually the alarm stopped. I never did find the cause; maybe the snow had blocked the air vents, as I'd also emptied the ashes out of the fire, and that might have been the source. Fortunately the snow didn't last long; it was all gone the next day, but it was pretty while it lasted.

We boated on, heading for Milton Keynes. Josh enjoyed it, partly because I fuelled him with promises of meals in pubs and talk of Jack Daniels whisky. He had a good time, and he got very proficient at boating. To start with he knew little about locks and swing bridges, but as time went on he became a very, very good crew member. I could send him up to a lock with the confidence that he knew what to do. He'd even sort out the other boaters if necessary – giving instructions, working out who were the beginners, and putting everybody straight if he needed to. It was useful to have someone to rely on, and also good for Josh as he has mild Asperger's

Syndrome and normally finds it difficult to deal with people.

Eventually we got to Cosgrove, near to Milton Keynes. As was becoming usual, I'd promised Josh a meal in the pub there, so we moored and walked into town. The pub, unfortunately, was closed for renovation. So I said, "Sorry, it's dad's cooking back on the boat I'm afraid" and we turned back. We'd hardly been gone any time at all, but when we got back to the boat there was a little note on it. It said, "Welcome to Cosgrove. This is a 48 hour mooring. We hope you'll be gone the day after tomorrow, Your Mooring Warden". Well! It was the most backhanded welcome I'd ever had to a place in my life! That was also my first introduction to the mooring standards of the south. It was totally different down there from my experiences further north; they were on your case all the time. I wasn't stopping in Cosgrove. Why would I - the pub was shut, and Milton Keynes beckoned.

Just after Milton Keynes the locks started. Out of the 102 on the Grand Union canal, 80 are between Milton Keynes and London, as the canal drops down into the Thames Valley. It's very intensive boating; we were doing about ten locks a day. One evening we got to Berkhampstead and began looking for a mooring for the night. We found a spot just outside a pub called *The Crystal Palace*; in fact we were right outside the front door which opened on to the towpath. We went in to see what they offered and there was a notice saying that they had an 'open mike night' on the Thursday; this was Monday. Josh, who's a keen musician, thought, "Ooo, I can play!" I agreed that we could stay, and he could indeed play. However, first we had to get his guitar, which he'd left back in Tamworth. So we left poor Cookie alone on the boat and caught the train back to Tamworth. It worried me leaving Cookie, but it worried me even more putting Josh on a train on his own; his Asperger's made it difficult for him to travel alone at that point...though he's much better now. The appointed date arrived and he made me play along with him on the flute, which I do play, but not particularly well. I remember that we played 'Stairway to Heaven' by Led Zeppelin. We got a round of applause, which was more than we deserved, because we were dreadful. Then someone asked, "Are you local? Have you got far to go home?", and I said, "About six feet". He looked at me a bit oddly, and I said, "I live there, on that boat". Cue the normal round of questions...

The next morning we left early, slipping off into the morning mist. Some of the locks were easier because we shared them with a group of boating boy scouts. They had a problem; their battery was flat, so I was able to give them a little help with that. In return neither Josh nor I had to touch a windlass or lock gate all day long. On this stretch of canal you can moor outside supermarkets; quite a few of them have their own moorings, and we parted company with the scouts at one of these as the opportunity to fill the cupboards was too good to miss. The locks on the Grand Union are famed for being difficult to operate, because the gates are heavy and tend to jam - although to be fair only once did I have to resort to ramming a lock gate open with 13 tons of *LadyRiverMouse*. This is not recommended but we had tried everything else. When we got to the last of the locks, even champion lock operator Josh thanked God that there were no more! And so it was that we boated across the viaduct over the North Circular Road and on into London.

By now Cookie had really got used to living on the boat. She took up what had become her normal cat routine. As soon as the engine started she would sit on the bunk in the back cabin, or on the floor. She would just curl up there and wait for the boat to stop moving. Whenever we got to a new place she'd come up and have a sniff and a look around. She usually decided that there had been dogs there and she wasn't going out, so then she'd go downstairs to her place again. I was very lucky in that Cookie had been an indoor cat before I had her and was used to that sort of life.

The main reason for the trip to London was to visit my sister Diane. As I already explained, Di had been instrumental in my getting the boat, and we wanted to see her to say hello. We moored a little way outside Paddington Basin, just before the weekend of the inland waterways boating festival. Arriving two days before the start of the festival, which was the bank holiday at the beginning of May, we were able to find a prime mooring in the middle of the festival site. Many other boats arrived, bedecked with flags and bunting and so on, and we were right in the thick of it. Di came down and joined me on the boat, and we had a good afternoon, picnicking on the deck and watching the parades of decorated boats. Even Cookie came up to have a look, but she decided that there were far too many people and went down below again.

Two days later they'd all gone – boats, people, flags, everything. Even Josh had gone back to the Midlands for a while, and it was just me and Cookie again. And two weeks after that I'd come to the end of my permitted time on that particular mooring, so I moved just around the corner into Paddington Basin itself. Paddington Basin is a big area of water, with lots of moorings. It used to be one of the main unloading docks for London. It's big enough to have moorings on pontoons and there are sanitary facilities a short distance away. It's a glorious mooring, right in the middle of the capital - but usually it's completely empty. The reason for this is that they have a strict '14 days and no return within a year' ruling, and there is a security guard there permanently, taking boat numbers. The result is that there's nobody there; all the people who can reach it easily have either had their 14 days or are saving them up for another time. It's a case of introducing a rule which has effectively stopped people using the facility which they've provided at great expense. Of course, they're trying to stop the Basin filling up with boaters who are living in what my sister called "the best address in London", but they've rather overdone it, because the result is that hardly anybody uses it at all. A bit crazy really. However, at the time of writing, the Canal and River Trust – a new body which took over from British Waterways – are introducing a new policy concerning mooring in Paddington Basin. I hope it helps people make better use of the facilities.

I was fine; I'd come from a long way off, so I was entitled to my 14 days and I used them. And not only is it a wonderfully convenient location, but because it has a security guard/mooring warden, it's secure as well. This meant that I was quite safe to leave Cookie on board while I went exploring London. I went to the Science Museum, the Natural History Museum, the Imperial War Museum, and the

Maritime Museum and Royal Observatory at Greenwich. I'd never really been a tourist in London but I was now and I took as much advantage as I could. I was somewhat limited because I was struggling even more with my health. I was now walking with a stick and tiring very easily, but by going out every other day and resting in between I saw most of the sights.

I was also having regular hospital appointments, and travelling back by train to keep them. I did this all the time while I was boating in fact, going to the hospital in Sutton Coldfield and to my GP in Tamworth. It was actually a bit of a bind, because I would have to plan to moor within reach of a railway station. I'd get there about two days early, because that's the sort of person I am, and I was never sure that I'd be able to find a safe mooring to leave *LadyRiverMouse* and her precious cargo of fluffy white cat. When I arrived I'd say to other boaters, "Hello, my name's David, and this is my cat, and the cat lives on board. So please be aware, if I'm not here and if the boat sinks or something, please get my cat off". As a result I started to be remembered as the person with the big white fluffy cat. Later on I would be approached by boaters who remembered sharing a mooring or a lock with us and who would always ask after "Cookie the fluffy white kitty".

My next long trip was planned to be along the Thames; out on to the tideway at Limehouse and upstream towards Reading and the Kennet and Avon. Ever since the Marchioness disaster in 1989, when the party boat *Marchioness* was rammed and sunk by the dredger *Bowbelle* with the loss of 51 lives, it has been compulsory for boats on the Thames to carry VHF radio. So for this next leg I needed a radio, and in order to operate it I needed a Marine Band VHF radio licence. For that I had to sit an exam, and to arrange that was going to take a little while. I did some research and found somewhere I could do the exams in London, but it was in around six weeks time. I'd already had my 14 days in Paddington Basin, so I had about six weeks to spend somewhere else in London.

So I set out along the Regents Canal; past Regents Park and the Snowden Aviary, which is all you can see of London Zoo from the canal. Thus I came to Camden Market and its lock. It was a lovely sunny day and there were hundreds of people sitting everywhere, leaning on the edges of lock, resting on the gates and balance beams, eating sandwiches and quaffing drinks. I had to more or less sweep them off the sides and gates. I opened the gate, went back to get the boat...and the gate shut itself. So I went back to the lock, opened the gate again and wedged it, went back...and the gate shut itself again. Meanwhile, not one of these people came to help me. There must have been dozens if not hundreds of them, but not a single one lifted a finger. "Can you help for a minute," I'd ask. And the replies were things like, "Oh no, I've never seen it move", or "I can't do that, I don't know if I'm allowed to". Very strange, London attitudes. Anyway, just as I was trying for a third time, another boat turned up. Hurray! We shared the lock, and all was well.

The other boat left me after a short while and I boated on alone through a London that only canal people see; backs of buildings, mostly covered in graffiti, lost dogs, and the occasional cyclist seeking refuge from the hustle and bustle of the streets. Then I came to a green area. This was Victoria Park. This oasis of green space is London's oldest public park and is in the East End area of Bethnal Green. I thought that this would do for a night. I was a little concerned about reports of crime in the area which were reinforced when I went to buy a newspaper and I was served through a security screen. My moorings, though, felt safe enough to stay another night, which led to another, then another, and before I knew it I had had my full two weeks. The only trouble I had was from the local squirrel population that will have a sandwich out of your hand as you are eating it! During this time a large steam fair assembled in the park and crowds of people came. I'm a bit of a steam engine fan so I went along, but what struck me most was the multicultural nature of the crowd. Almost every group of people seemed to be of a different nationality or culture, rubbing along together, united by the single desire to have fun and a good time. This show of inter cultural solidarity cheered me even more than the fun and spectacle of the fairground.

I had to move on, and next came the River Lea via the very short Hertford Union Canal. I still had a month until my radio course so was looking for somewhere to stop for a while. So I came to Tottenham, and I spent quite a long time there, several weeks in fact. There were good reasons for this. I'd barely tied the ropes when a young girl came over to talk to me: "Welcome to Tottenham, welcome to the boating community, are you stopping long? The safest place to moor is over there; come up and join us in our mooring community". I thought that was really nice; I'd only been there about five minutes, and I wondered if I'd found my month's stopping place. They turned out to be a lovely group of people – four or five boats, kids, chickens etc.

They spent their time dodging mooring wardens, while living peacefully in Tottenham. They loved Cookie and thought she was wonderful. In the time I was in Tottenham, three youths were stabbed to death in the town, but I just had nothing but smiles and welcomes from everybody.

It was while I was in Tottenham that I broke a lock! Well, I didn't really. Up until then I'd been moored below Stonebridge Lock while the rest of the community were above the lock. I decided that I wanted the extra security of being moored with the other boaters, so I moved *LadyRiverMouse* into the lock. The locks on the Lea are mechanised so all the boater has to do is press the appropriate buttons and it all works like magic. Only on this occasion I pressed the button...and the gates moved halfway and stopped. The hydraulic system had run out of oil. It was Sunday so I didn't have much hope when I called the emergency British Waterways number, but just as I was thinking that I'd have to spend a night on board stuck at the bottom of the lock, a van arrived with two engineers and a drum of oil. The community used to joke for quite a while afterwards: "David, have you broken our lock?" sort of thing, but it was all in good fun.

While I was in Tottenham I finally managed to do the radio course. I left Cookie on board *LadyRiverMouse* under the watchful eye of the other boaters, who had now become friends, and caught a tube to The Strand, where a sailing school had rented a room for the day. There were about a dozen students, but I was the only narrowboater; all the others seemed to be from the yachting fraternity. We spent the morning studying the theory and the afternoon making practice radio calls on dummy sets and checking that we all knew the NATO phonetic alphabet which we had all been asked to learn in advance. Then there was the exam. We all passed and were declared fully qualified marine radio operators. I stopped off in Tottenham Court Road on the way back to buy a suitable radio. I was now fully equipped for the next leg.

It was now July, so university holidays, and Josh came back to join me for the next stage. Di joined me as well, just for the trip up the tidal Thames as far as Richmond, a one day trip. We were delayed for a day as the lock keeper said that the water was too rough. This stretch of river is challenging and not to be taken lightly; as a boater, you can insist on going, but you'd be a fool to do so! I looked at the water on the other side of the lock, and it was going up and down about four or five feet. I decided the lock keeper was spot on, and we'd wait and see what happened the next day. The lock keepers are really, really good; they know what boats will do, and they know how long it takes, and where you're going, and they look out for you all the way up the Thames.

The next day the lock keeper said it was OK; it was still pretty choppy but we'd be alright. We donned our lifejackets, which I'd bought for the trip, turned on the VHF radio to listen to the traffic on the water, slipped into the lock, and then with an audience of dozens of onlookers, we went out into the Thames. Narrowboats do go out on to the Thames but rarely enough that when one does it attracts a crowd. The gates opened; no paddles on these, the lock keeper opens them slowly, and when he thinks he can, he opens them the rest of the way. They're big hydraulically operated gates, and its really powerful stuff. I'd already put Cookie in her cat carrier for this trip; there was no way I was risking having her jump out into the Thames. We bucked and tossed a bit, and then I got used to it and I saw that *LadyRiverMouse* was quite happy in the waves. We weren't rolling at all; we pitched a little, but she was really very stable. There was movement, as you would expect, but it was fine. Then Di came up and told me there was an awful smell down below. The toilet tank had been well stirred up by the movement of the boat. I handed the tiller over to Josh for a moment, went down below, and put a big black bin bag over the toilet, which solved the problem nicely.

It takes five hours to get to Richmond lock on the rising tide. You have the speed of the engine and of the tide, but even so, it's quite a long way. We sailed under Tower Bridge, and London Bridge; we went past the Houses of Parliament, remembering to keep well away from them otherwise you attract unwanted attention by the security forces, or so they say. It was a glorious afternoon. Di even produced sandwiches which she'd brought. The light was fading as we arrived at Richmond lock; it was around 9 pm. but the lock keeper was waiting for us; as I said, they knew what time to expect us. It was a very tired crew that passed through on to the non-tidal part of the Thames, and I was very grateful to tie up after a long day, then to walk back and pay the mooring fee. On the Thames and indeed most rivers you pay for moorings; here it was only a few pounds. Later I would find that moorings on the Thames can be far more expensive. And so it was that I left London...

Chapter 7
Winter in Newbury

My plan was to head for the Kennet and Avon canal, and Newbury in particular. There was a reason for this. I'd been sharing my adventures by letter with a very old childhood friend, someone I hadn't seen for years. Mandy and I had been at school together more years ago than either of us cared to remember, and had kept in touch ever since. I knew that she wanted to see *LadyRiverMouse* and Cookie, but she had had a very nasty road accident which had left her unable to travel far; and in any case she couldn't leave her eleven border collies for longer than an afternoon. So I'd decided that I would go and see her. Newbury was as close as I could get to where she lived, so that's where I was now heading.

I loved boating along rivers. The Thames was a delight; wide, clean and with something new to see around every corner. However, I had one major issue with it. People don't go out boating on the Thames, what they do is go out mooring! They leave very early in the morning, in their very flash boats, all polished teak and brass, and they moor up somewhere conspicuous and show everybody what they've got. So if you haven't found a mooring by about midday, you're more or less scuppered – all the moorings are full. I did find places; usually as I boated late into the afternoon some of the day moorers would be heading home. But on a couple of occasions I had to resort to tying *LadyRiverMouse* to trees. My plan of last resort was to drop the anchor in midstream but I never had to resort to that.

It was lovely boating, going upstream. It was just these 'Hooray Henrys' who were the problem. The locks were big, and had lock keepers. In a way this made it easier but in another way it was much harder. The lock keepers motion you in; they know how many boats they can fit into their big wide locks, and all sensible lock keepers will get the narrowboats in first. This is because we're big, heavy and made of steel. A narrowboat will cut through a fibreglass 'gin palace' without even a sound, so their plan is to get the narrowboats in and stationary, then fit in the other craft around them. Then powerful motors close the gates and open the paddles. The water swirls in forming eddies and undercurrents, and as the boats rise, the crews hold them with ropes. This is a problem for lone narrowboaters, and though Josh was with me at this time, he was often still in bed if I was boating in the morning. Controlling a boat on just a single centreline is difficult if not impossible in these circumstances, but without having arms 50 feet long there is little choice. On one occasion I incurred the wrath of a lock keeper by doing this, but as I pointed out, what else could I do. On another occasion *LadyRiverMouse* began to move away from the lock side towards another vessel, a very highly polished one, and somebody on it called out in a posh accent, "You'll hit my boat". I looked and decided that there was actually plenty of space so I rather off handedly replied, "I'm not bothered; I don't suppose it'll cause me much damage". I didn't mean to be unkind, but there really was plenty of room. What worried me most was rowing boats going through locks next to us - up to eight people, sometimes young children, in skiffs with precious little freeboard. You know that if you make a wrong move you'll tip them over, and the people in them will end up in the water in the maelstrom below.

Then there were those who couldn't handle their boats properly. When we were below Maidenhead lock waiting for the boats coming down, I tied up, and a chap behind me in a big fibreglass cruiser just went round in a circle, then did it again, and then a third time. Eventually we all went into the lock, and I asked him what he'd been doing. He said, "I'm not very good at tying up". On the Thames the standard of boating is abysmal...but the standard of polishing is first rate. In fact the rule seems to be that the shinier the boat the less competent the crew. I was very grateful that we didn't sink anyone.

I encountered another slight problem on the Thames. In the locks you have to turn your engine off. This is a sensible rule and prevents nasty toxic exhaust fumes building up in the confines of the lock. However, *LadyRiverMouse's* engine didn't like starting when it was hot; Bertha, as I named the engine, would always start from cold, but when hot the starter motor would jam. Eventually, with enough flicks of the switch, it would go, but it could take a few minutes, and the lock keepers always want to get the next people in. In the end I'd leave the engine running, unless the lock keeper absolutely demanded that it be turned off.

The chaos reached a peak as we approached Henley. It was regatta week and there were numerous rowing boats all over the river. I boated up through the course in *LadyRiverMouse* while the rowers tried their best to get under our bows. There was a little lane to one side for normal river traffic, which we were in, but some of the rowers just saw this as an additional practice area. This was dangerous; there was at least one occasion when a rowing eight very nearly became two rowing fours! I found a place to moor, right in the middle of the event, but there was a price to pay - £35. I paid this at a little pay and display machine on the bank. I stuck the little ticket in a window, but that didn't stop us being woken in the morning by the mooring warden. He was apologetic when I sleepily pointed to my ticket; however, very few boaters use the machine to pay so he comes round to collect the fees directly. My highly priced mooring in Henley did, however, give me an excellent view of the boating traffic. While I sat and watched, I was aware that the boat immediately next to us on the mooring was receiving a large number of packages brought along the towpath on a sack truck. All contained alcohol of some description. Ah, maybe some of the erratic boating was explained! This was confirmed by the lock keeper at Henley as he waved us through early the next morning: "Drunk as skunks most of them".

The first thing that greets the boater turning off the Thames on to the Kennet and Avon at Reading is a red light. Traffic lights are rare on the waterways but here, through the Octagon Centre in Reading, the navigation is narrow and twisting and the current is ferocious. There is no room to pass an oncoming boat and no way to stop; hence the traffic light control. This is just the first taste of the joys of the Kennet and Avon. Things are complicated here. Every lock is different, and the river enters at strange points below locks. There are cross currents and blind bends. There are swing bridges that are timed so that they can only be opened once every 20 minutes, as there are 'A' roads above them. Some locks have scalloped sides and yet others have no sides at all; these are the famed 'turf sided' locks, the sides of the lock chamber being just a grassy bank.

There's one place on the Kennet where all these horrors come together. A swing bridge, then a blind bend, followed by a lock entrance with a vicious cross current running across it. It's really quite tricky, with nowhere to stop if things go wrong. For the lone boater the nightmare is that having set everything up, with lock gates and swing bridge open, some well meaning person closes one of them before you can get through. Fortunately I had a crew when I went through it. I sent Josh up to open the lock gates; then I opened the bridge. Quickly casting off and opening the throttle wide, I sent *LadyRiverMouse* scooting up through the current and into the lock. I didn't even touch the sides, and someone on the bank said, " Good God, you must have done that before". But of course I'd never been there before in my life.

Several months later, going downsteam was even harder, because I had the river pushing me down, and there's a tiny little landing stage to stop at to close the bridge again. If you miss the landing stage, it's about two miles before you can find a place to stop. I saw someone get off here with his centreline, and his boat swung across the river and very nearly sank. Eventually this boater had to let go and catch the boat further downstream. The Kennet was full of this kind of hazard. I said at the time, and I still say, that if you can boat from Reading or Newbury or back again then you can call yourself a narrowboater. For my part I began to think that I seemed to have been born with something of the ability to handle a boat. It wasn't that I always found things easy – far from it. But I seemed to learn quickly, and once I'd encountered a difficult situation, it didn't bother me the second time around. I'm exceedingly grateful for this skill, as apart from the times when I did stupid things, I never had any real trouble with boat handling throughout all my years of cruising.

When we finally arrived in Newbury, Josh left and went back to his mother's. It was now August, and he had to get ready to return to university in September. I had arranged to see Mandy as planned, but this would now have to wait. For the very day I arrived in Newbury, Mandy's elderly mother fell and broke her hip, and seeing to her mum in hospital was taking all Mandy's time. However, for now I had no other plans, so I decided to stay in Newbury for a while. It would also give me a break after several weeks of fairly intensive boating. Next day I was filling up with diesel at Greenham Island Boat Services and I mentioned to the proprietor that I was looking for a mooring for a little while. He offered me a month at a reasonable rate which included electricity, so I took it.

Cookie seemed to like Greenham Boat Services and she spent some time happily wandering ashore, but one day she met the resident shore cat. They had a bit of an altercation, or to be more accurate, a real fight. Poor white fluffball Cookie has always been more of a decorative cat and not really made for fighting, although that doesn't stop her trying. She came home with a wound which obviously needed some attention. I knew nothing of

Newbury, having just arrived, so I quickly googled 'Vets in Newbury', found the nearest one and took her there. It was lucky I did, as she was developing an abscess. The young vet I saw tried to drain it and sent me away with some antibiotics. I attempted to bathe it as she'd told me to, but it was a deep puncture wound and I just couldn't keep it open and draining. Another vet appointment was required. This time Cookie saw a different vet, and I suspect he was more experienced. He opened up the wound, cleaned it out thoroughly, and gave her yet more antibiotics. This time it worked and she started to recover. It was only a bit of an infection really, but it was a worry, as Cookie is very, very important to me. To be fair to shore cats this one wasn't particularly nasty; it just thought this bit of Greenham Island was its own territory and not Cookie's. It actually wasn't even a real shore cat; it lived on a boat and it used one of the portholes as a cat flap, jumping in and out that way. Later on this boat turned out to be there illegally and they got moved on, but that's another story.

Mandy did come and see me eventually and we had lunch together on *LadyRiverMouse*. It was good to meet up with her. She had been a great help to me following my cancer diagnosis, suggesting all sorts of alternative therapies, most of which I tried at some time or another. It's easy to be critical of these things but none was very expensive and any one might have worked. It may be that I was clutching at straws but as the conventional medics had all but written me off I thought that I had nothing to lose and everything to gain.

When my month was up I left Greenham Boat Services, but I didn't go far – just to West Mills, which is on the outskirts of the town and still really part of Newbury. I was kind of wondering what to do. How far should I go along the Kennet and Avon? I'd done all I set out to do, ie been to London and seen my sister, and then met Mandy. I didn't really want to do that much more at the moment; I had a very ambitious scheme to go out to sea at Bristol and up the Severn Estuary; but that would take a lot of planning and maybe even some work to make *LadyRiverMouse* more seaworthy. So while I thought about this I decided that I would stick around in the area, just moving the boat when I needed to.

To keep myself busy I bought a project for the winter from a model shop. This was *Calypso*, a model boat which I proceeded to build over the next couple of months. I love model making, and I thought that this would keep me occupied over the winter. Calypso is a model of Jack Cousteau's research vessel from the 1960s and 70s, which had featured on almost everyone's TV screens at that time. It is a metre long, half a metre high, and took up a lot of space. I still have that boat – and it still takes up a lot of space! At one stage I taped black plastic all over the cabin so that I could turn it into a spray booth for spraying the model's hull. Now, that's something you can only do if you live on your own.

I also took up photography. I'd dabbled with cameras and lenses way back in the days of 35mm film and it seemed an ideal hobby to get back into, especially as digital cameras would take up very little space on the boat. As a result I started posting my pictures on the Flickr website where they still are– at www.flickr.com/photos/ladyrivermouse/.

After I'd been in West Mills a little while I started to attract the attention of the mooring wardens of course. It took a little longer than I expected, but as promised long before by the lady with the chickens whom I'd met way back near Husbands Bosworth, they did catch up with me. To be fair I had been on a 14 day mooring for a month, so it was reasonable to give me notice to move on. What wasn't so reasonable was the timing, as by this time a rather harsh winter had frozen the canal solid, and moving was not possible. I phoned them up and told them this, and they said, "Well, when you can, move". This might have been possible earlier than it was if the locks in both directions hadn't been closed and drained for maintenance. This work overran due to the harshness of the winter and it was nearly Easter before I could continue my trip. In the way of bureaucracies everywhere, British Waterways kept up the regular flow of notices. Each time I'd phone and be given the 'move when you can' line - but at least the notices provided me with a ready supply of firelighters!

The towpath we were moored on was a favourite route into Newbury for shoppers and I got to know a few folk quite well. During this time Cookie took to sitting out on deck, and one afternoon I heard a child's voice: "Mummy Mummy look at that great big FAT cat". Cookie had never been thin, but after this I looked at her more objectively and decided that a diet was in order. In fact I'd put on a couple of extra pounds too. So it was the start of a new regime for both of us, which would last on and off for the rest of our time on board and beyond.

Eventually the thaw came and I moved up to Kintbury lock. Kintbury is a nice little village five minutes from Newbury's shops and facilities – that is by sensible means of transport like trains and cars, as it's a couple of hours on a boat. It was not a very satisfactory mooring; the main visitor moorings were the other side of the lock which remained closed for maintenance and I had to use a plank to get ashore. Now, you get all sorts of debris building up between the boat and the bank, especially when there's work taking place on the lock only a few yards away, and diesel and oil and so on are getting spilled into the water. All this nasty, oily water was gathering between the boat and the bank, under the plank. I said the fateful words to Cookie, "Whatever you do, don't fall in there".

Five minutes later, in comes a wet, oily, filthy Cookie-cat. She'd fallen in of course. She'd managed to get out of the watery slime on to the bank with no problems as it was a grassy slope and she traipsed the resulting drippy mess back indoors. Yuck! It took several days to get her back to her usual white fluffiness, but we got there in the end. It was two more weeks before the maintenance team finished work on the lock and it was finally declared open. *LadyRiverMouse* was the first boat through.

As I boated on I was always on the lookout for potential mooring sites. The mooring wardens on the Kennett & Avon are keen on their work, as you will have gathered, so it was with some surprise that I sailed past a boat that looked as if it had been there for some time. There was even a landing stage of sorts. Always one to be curious and to find any loopholes in the system, I tied up nearby and knocked on the boat. A tall woman rose from the cabin and offered a hand: "Hello, I'm Natasha and I'm just recovering from my sex change operation". Well as an opening line that had me floored for a moment, but then we had quite a long chat. Natasha told me about her problems and history; and a sorry tale it was of depression and persecution. I eventually found out the part relevant to boating - that she had been given special dispensation for a limited time for the mooring until she was fully recovered. However, don't think that the mooring wardens had an attack of compassion; this sort of thing is allowed for in the legislation under a medical exemption – although few boaters need it for a sex change.

I had got as far as Great Bedwyn when I got the message which sends fear into every parent's heart. My daughter Lizzie had been rushed into hospital with a severe complication of tonsillitis known as quinsy. Lizzie was not a child any more, but of course I still wanted to see her as soon as I could. Luckily I had kept my car with me throughout the winter and it was parked in Great Bedwyn railway station car park. So I put Cookie into her carrier, secured *LadyRiverMouse* as best I could and headed for the Midlands. My mother lives near Nuneaton and Cookie and I stayed there for a few days while I visited Lizzie, who was receiving intravenous antibiotics in Burton-on-Trent hospital, which is only a short drive. Quinsy can have serious complications including death, so I was very relieved when she started to recover.

Eventually she was discharged from hospital and Cookie and I could return to our peripatetic life. On the way back to the boat I was treated to the wonderful sight of a barn owl. I was driving along the little lane to Great Bedwyn when the huge bird silently swooped down in front of the car. It flew on as I drove - only a few feet from my side window, veering off eventually into a patch of woodland. Not all magical experiences happen while actually on the water.

It was March 2009. I could now, finally, start boating again.

Waiting for the lock to reopen after the winter maintenance programme had overrun at Kintbury. This is where Cookie fell from the gangplank into the oily sludge between the bank and the boat.

Chapter 8
Cruising to Wales

I set out initially towards Bath and Bristol. I still wanted to go through Bristol on to the Severn Estuary and up the coast to Gloucester. However, it would be very expensive, and I would need to have work done on the boat - since I would effectively be taking her to sea I would have to have the engine room made a lot more watertight. I would also need to have a pilot on board. Pilots normally only guide large ships into harbour, but in amongst the constantly shifting sandbanks and unpredictable currents of the Severn Estuary I would have to have this expert help too. And it would also mean a lot of hard boating even before that. So I was actually somewhat apprehensive about the whole thing.

In fact, I gave up the idea fairly early on. When I got to the top of the Caen Hill flight in Devizes, and I looked down at the 27 locks of the flight, I thought to myself, "I can't do this". It all seemed like too much. I was on my own. It would be three or four days of hard work, at the end of which I would still be within easy walking distance of where I'd started from. When I really considered my ambitious plan, I just didn't want to do it. I'd also made a half promise to Josh to take *LadyRiverMouse* to Oxford, where one of his university friends lived, to show off our floating home. I made up my mind; time for a change of plan. I turned round and set off back towards Reading and the Thames. I would pick up Josh on the way and we would call in at Oxford, but our real destination was to be North Wales. Why? Well, I hadn't been there, and why not?

I should mention that I had a wonderful time in Devizes; it was a lovely town. While I was there a strange thing happened. I was strolling about in the sunshine when a complete stranger asked me if I was blind. I thought at first that I had got in his way in some inconsiderate manner but in fact this chap was serious. He was partially sighted himself and had just made out my camera lens and thought it was a seeing lens such as the one he used himself. He then insisted on showing me round his home town. It was rather strange having a registered blind guide, but I had a very pleasant and informative time.

I picked up Josh as I passed through Pewsey, which he had managed to reach by himself, and we boated together back along the route we had travelled the previous summer as far as Reading; there we turned upstream through Abingdon and went on to Oxford. The Thames was the same mix of huge boats and semi-competent boaters that I remembered. However, I shouldn't be too critical as at one of the locks on the approach to Oxford I got in a bit of a tangle myself. An orange light indicated that there was no lock keeper on duty and that we would have to work the lock ourselves. Josh was below in the cabin as I brought *LadyRiverMouse* alongside the rather narrow jetty below the lock, where we would tie up and begin to operate the lock. As I stepped on to the jetty holding the mooring rope, I suddenly realised that the current from the weir was flowing under the raised walkway and pushing *LadyRiverMouse* away from me. The force was terrific and I only just managed to get a turn of the rope around a bollard to prevent the boat being swept away. I have no idea what I would have done if I had been on my own, but just as I was starting to panic Josh appeared on the deck and I was able to shout across for him to use the engine to regain control. No harm was done in the end, but it was a reminder of how quickly things can go wrong if you let your concentration lapse, and also just how powerful the river can be.

At Oxford the river changed character completely. Osney Bridge was too low for anything much taller than a narrowboat, and within a only a few yards the atmosphere went from busy waterway full of trip boats and gin palaces to laid back stream of punts and rowing boats. We reached Kidlington, just north of Oxford, and tied up there. I spent two peaceful weeks while Josh and his friend partied the nights away in the town.

Here as in most places Cookie didn't venture out much because of the number of dogs on the towpath. The fact that they were on leads and sometimes smaller than her didn't figure in her thinking at all – dogs were to be avoided. It was not the same with birds. Any bird no matter how big was fair game. People feed the ducks, which encourages them to become braver, and unfortunately this also applies to swans. Swans are big powerful birds with lots of attitude, a huge hiss, and a vicious beak to back it up. You don't mess with swans. But Cookie didn't seem to think that way. One afternoon she and I were soaking up the sun on deck when a swan swam up and began to crane its long neck over the edge looking for dropped crumbs. Cookie was not amused at this interloper; quick as a flash a white paw streaked out and she slapped the huge bird on the side of its beak. The swan was completely taken aback; it just swam away with its whole being radiating a 'that didn't happen' aura. For Cookie, small dogs meant she should run away. Huge birds – bring it on...

Our route to North Wales took us through the infamous Harecastle tunnel. As I have probably already mentioned, no boater really likes tunnels. They are dark, cold, damp, soulless places at best but at Harecastle you can add claustrophobia to the mix. The tunnel roof has subsided in places to only inches above a narrowboat roof and it is only wide enough for a single boat. For this reason a one way system operates, controlled by two tunnel keepers. There is one more peculiarity - because the bore is so small, the air is kept clear of noxious fumes by enormous fans situated in a room above the south portal, and to assist with the airflow there are doors across the canal.

It was a bright sunny day when Josh, Cookie and I arrived on *LadyRiverMouse* at the south entrance and I wandered over to the tunnel keeper's office to find out how long we would have to wait. There were three boats in the tunnel ahead of us, and it seemed that after that we could go. There was just long enough to complete the paperwork really - name and number of boat, number of crew, any dogs... All dogs have to be restrained in some way while on boats in the tunnel in case they take it into their heads to jump off and swim for it. They didn't mention cats, but I realised that Cookie would have to go in her carrier for the trip. I was given a run down on the emergency drill - basically a system of horn codes for use if we broke down halfway through. I couldn't remember when I had last used the horn so I made a mental note to check that it was working before setting off.

As I sat waiting in the sunshine the tunnel keeper appeared from his office and opened the tunnel doors. Within seconds the first boat entered, followed closely by the other two, and then he signalled to us to enter. As we slipped through the entrance the doors closed behind us and we had a second or two to adjust to the darkness, now only illuminated by the lights on *LadyRiverMouse*. Then the ventilation fans started up with an almighty roar that completely drowned out the engine. I was ready for this but I was completely unprepared for what came next. The fans create a low pressure zone in the tunnel which in its turn causes the moisture in the air to turn to a cold mist. This fog then rushes down the tunnel towards the boats entering from the south. Every canal tunnel has its ghost stories and after experiencing this phenomenon I could see where they came from. It certainly spooked me for a moment.

We had travelled 100 yards or so when the noise of the fans stopped and a light behind showed that the entrance doors had been opened. A silhouette in the light showed that another boat was following us through the tunnel. Then, as the doors closed and the fans restarted, the now familiar fog swept past once more - but I was ready for it this time. Then the tunnel roof got lower and lower. In places sudden changes in height were marked in white paint. At its lowest there were only inches of clearance above the roof. It was fortunate that I had taken the chimney down as there was definitely not room for it, and in fact I had to crouch down at the tiller to avoid hitting my head on the roof. It took about an hour and a half for the passage.

As we came out we found that the weather had changed completely. In contrast to the bright sunshine we had left, we emerged into a Kidsgrove of gloom and heavy rain. This rain continued on and off for our entire descent of 'Heartbreak Hill', as the locks which take the Trent and Mersey down from the summit at Harecastle to the Cheshire plain are generally known. The locks here are duplicated so that there are two to choose from, but that didn't stop just about every one being set against us, so that we had to stop and fill each lock before we used it. At one of these, Josh demonstrated that he could not only work locks but could handle *LadyRiverMouse* rather well too. It was my turn to work the locks and Josh was steering. As I prepared one of the locks a sudden gust of wind blew *LadyRiverMouse* into a most difficult position. I couldn't see how Josh could get her into the lock – it needed a sharp double turn and there just wasn't the room. I shouted for him to throw me a rope to use to guide the boat in, but Josh was confident and just opened the throttle. I closed my eyes and waited for the bang but when I opened them...lo and behold, *LadyRiverMouse* was gliding perfectly into the lock. To this day I have no idea how he did it – I'm sure I couldn't have managed it.

The weather improved as we made our way through Middlewich and on to the Llangollen canal at Hurleston. It was at about this point that I became aware that the engine didn't seem to be its usual happy self. There was nothing very specific; just a slightly different sound. When I looked at it I just thought that maybe a rubber engine mounting was getting weak.　However, there was a convenient boatyard at Maestermyn, just beyond Ellesmere, and I stopped here to get an engineer to check out my suspicions.　He had a good look but pronounced everything to be fine.　So I believed him and carried on.

It was August when we sailed across the famous Pontcysyllte aqueduct and into Llangollen. When I asked Josh later where his favourite place had been, this was it.　It is indeed a lovely spot, although a supermarket near the canal would have been useful. We stayed for a few days but then had to start making our way back.　So we left late one evening with the aim of travelling over the aqueduct in the dark.　There are no specific rules that ban boating at night, although most hire boat firms forbid it, and we just thought that it would be a fun thing to do.　It did indeed give a different view - one of lights spread out right across the valley.　I expect that the lights of *LadyRiverMouse* sailing across the sky gave a few people something to look at too!

One of the most noticable things about the Llangollen Canal is the large number of hire boats crewed by novice holidaymakers.　These people have been sold a dream of a tranquil holiday floating through the countryside between welcoming inns and hostelries, which is sometimes very far from the truth. At New Marton Bottom lock an incident occurred with demonstrates just how ill prepared some of these families are...

As we approached the lock I was pleased to see, even from a distance, that the lock was set for us; that is it was full of water and the gates were open ready for us to sail straight in.　As we got nearer, however,　a young family appeared　on foot from below the lock. They closed the gates and made to empty the water out to allow their own boat in. This is the boating equivalent of slamming the door in someone's face! Downright rude doesn't come into it; it's wasteful of water, makes more work for yourself, and just ISN'T DONE! I was too far away to shout, but I sounded *LadyRiverMouse*'s horn just to make sure that these folk knew we were there - but to no effect whatsoever.

Normally I would go up and help folk operate a lock. But I was feeling peeved, so I just tied *'Mouse* to the lock mooring and sat and watched. Soon, though, events took a dangerous turn. Dad and little daughter were attempting to operate the paddles with their windlass, but they released the ratchet which restrains the mechanism without taking the L shaped handle off the spindle first. The effect of this was that the heavy windlass spun round at high speed, left the spindle, and swung through the air – missing the little girl's ear by centimetres. I was horrified! It wasn't that these people were rude; they just didn't know what they were doing. I called Josh and we went forward to give a lesson in how to safely operate 200 year old lock machinery, and as an aside we mentioned a bit of canal etiquette too. It turned out that they had only just picked up their boat from a hire base and had received no tuition except for a small pamphlet on how to operate a lock. Needless to say they were very grateful for our help, and I hoped that they had a good holiday. It could easily have ended in tragedy there that afternoon.

Next I had in mind that I would go and visit my old friend Jeff, who lived by the canal near Coventry and whose house I'd passed in the pouring rain on the way to London. But I never made it. As I reached Penkridge, near Cannock, the engine began to sound much, much worse. It was grinding and making a horrible noise, and was obviously not aligned properly with the propeller shaft. Luckily there was a boatyard in Penkridge, so I stopped there. The guy running it came out, and he just said, "Oh dear; you have a problem". The engine block had cracked right across and the whole thing had slipped and dropped into the bilges. I was amazingly lucky that it was still running at all.

It was time to bite the bullet. I still hadn't had the work done that the surveyor had identified when I'd bought the boat, and some things were getting worse. After all, it hadn't seemed that urgent; I'd never even expected to live this long! I'd thought I'd be boating for a couple of years, not for as long as this. It was time to have everything done. I needed a new engine, I needed plating on the engine room, and I wanted quite a lot of other work done; the engine room vents moved for a start so that rain water no longer drained into them. I also wanted a larger engine room hatch, new tiller bearings, and an improved exhaust. While the boat was out of the water it could have the routine maintenance also - the stuff that a boat has to have done every two or three years. Overall, it was time to lift *LadyRiverMouse* out of the water and give her a thorough seeing to.

It was now September and Josh needed to go back to university. Anyway, there was no point in him staying with me if we weren't doing any boating. And it looked as if I'd be in Penkridge for quite a while. In fact, they were very good to me in that boatyard. They ran me back to Tamworth to pick up my car and connected *LadyRiverMouse* to an electricity supply, which was very useful, particularly as it was three weeks before they could fit me in to do the work, and another three or four weeks work on the boat would be required. I carried on living on the boat with Cookie while we were waiting for the work to begin. Cookie was OK. She was a bit wary of boatyards by now because she thought they might have fierce cats in them but she did venture out. Cookie always knew that she lived on a boat but quite often couldn't remember which one and once I found her once sitting on one of the new boats next to mine, the brand new ones that were ready to be sold. She looked as though she was saying, "Can we have this one please".

It became more difficult when they hoisted us out on to the bank, to actually start the work. I had a ladder to get on board, but Cookie took one look at this and decided she was going indoors and staying there. This was fine until the really noisy stuff started. There was hammering, welding, grinding, and dust - and Cookie didn't like it at all. So I took her and went to live with my mum for a few days while that kind of work was being done. I couldn't have Cookie living on board with all that dust and noise; and it was good to get away from it myself.

Finally it was all done, and done well. And I'll never ever grumble about a garage bill ever again after that one. It came to a shade short of 15 grand. I always tell people that living on a boat is not a cheap option. People think it's an inexpensive way of living, but it's not. OK, you don't have a council tax bill to pay, but you do have a licence fee, which is just about the same amount. You don't pay a great deal for your electricity – but you don't get very much, and you have to generate it yourself. Per unit, it costs about 300 times the amount to generate it yourself than you could buy it from the national grid. You've still got heating bills; the only reason they're less is because the living space is tiny. And you've got these enormous maintenance bills at intervals because your home is sitting in water all the time – and the water will find a way in eventually. You've constantly got to be emptying your toilet. You've got to sort out your own facilities, or stay in a marina and pay for theirs. It really isn't a cheap way of life; you've got to want to do it for it to be worth it. I met a landlord of a pub near Newbury who hated boaters with a passion, which is rather bizarre as he relied on them for 90% of his trade. But he thought they were a bunch of spongers and scroungers who didn't pay council tax. What he ignored was that they were paying at least as much in licence fees to maintain the water which ran past his picturesque pub and brought him holiday makers and people to spend money in his bar. I tried to explain all this to him when I was there but to no effect.

However, if you do like boating, it's worth every penny. There's a marvellous freedom which comes from being self sufficient and not attached to the power and water companies. This only goes so far as you are still of course reliant on shore supplies of gas, diesel, coal, water etc, but at least you can pretend to be a lone independent soul. Then there is the other type of freedom - if you don't like a place or you fall out with the neighbours it is only the work of a moment to cast off and be somewhere else. For my part I never tired of opening the curtains in the morning to a view of the water, with not a sound except the wind in the trees, the lapping ripples, and quacks from ducks swimming by.

Anyway, it was now October and all the work

had been done. I could finally resume my interrupted plans. However, just as I was about to set off, I got a message to say that Jeff had died. I felt really, really dreadful. I hadn't seen him on the way to London because the weather had been so bad, and then of course I'd got tied up in Penkridge. If the engine hadn't failed I'd have made it. Someone once said that 'if only' were the two saddest words in the English language, and at this point I really agreed.

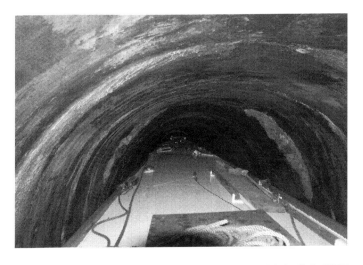

Inside Harecastle tunnel. You can see that I have laid the little VHF aerial flat on the roof which gets even lower than this in places.

Chapter 9
Winter in Alvecote

I tried out my new engine on the way from Penkridge back to Tamworth, and it ran beautifully. It was going to give me a couple of nasty moments later, but I didn't know that at the time. I didn't want to spend another six months fighting mooring wardens, so I went for the legal option and booked a mooring at Alvecote Marina, near Tamworth, for the winter. Alvecote is between Tamworth and the little town of Polesworth where Cookie had fallen in the water so long ago. Wet lost cats aside, Polesworth is a lovely town with a very well stocked second hand bookshop in which I spent a lot of time. I thought everything would be fine, and that I'd just hole up for the winter.

Unfortunately it didn't turn out like that. While I was in the marina I'd stopped boating, and I didn't realise how much that would affect me, how much boating had been holding me together. It was grey, it was cold, and it was miserable. Everything caught up with me in a big way. It came to me that I'd lost my parent, I'd lost my house, I'd lost my family, I'd lost my health, one after another. I'd lost everything! And finally I'd just lost one of my oldest friends. Looking back, I think it was Jeff's death which finally precipitated this state; it was the last straw. The marina had seemed like a good idea at the time but it didn't really work for me; rather than a safe haven I felt trapped and isolated. All the colour drains out of the world when you're depressed, so I'm not sure how grey Alvecote is compared with anywhere else, but it seemed it. So there I was, sitting in a boat in a marina and everything had caught up with me. I didn't know it, but I had a bad case of clinical depression. All I realised at the time was that I felt miserable and helpless.

Eventually it was Jane, who I still saw sometimes and who happened to be visiting, who dragged me along to see the nurse at the GP's surgery. The nurse asked me what was wrong and I just burst into tears. They gave me a form to fill in on how well I was feeling. The maximum score of 'depressedness' is 30 - I scored 27. The nurse told me that I needed to see a doctor, and as soon as possible. She must have really meant it, because she got on the computer and rescheduled everyone's appointments, and then told me that I was next. The doctor gave me anti-depressants with a warning that things would get worse before they got better. He also gave me two phone numbers; one was the mental health emergency call-out number, and the other was the Samaritans. He told me to go home, but if I needed help, I could phone either of these numbers 24 hours a day.

He was right about things getting worse initially. I finally did something which I never thought I would do in a million years - I phoned the Samaritans. I spoke to a girl called Ellie who was lovely. I remember that she had a thick black country accent, so it was a good thing I had worked in that part of the world and understood the language. She chatted to me for a bit, but I just couldn't see any point in going on; all I could see in the future was misery and a messy end.

Then, in the middle of the conversation, Cookie came in and sat on my knee, going "purr, purr, purrrrr". Suddenly things looked brighter. I said to Ellie, "It's alright now, my cat's come in. I'll be alright now that I've got my cat". Cookie really did make that much of a difference to me. It might sound crazy, but she was the love of my life right then, and it is not going too far to say that she saved my life that night.

As the pills started to work, things gradually began to improve. I visited local parks and took *LadyRiverMouse* on a few short trips, and slowly the colour started to return to the world. However, all this had made me realise that I had a huge decision to make. While I was happy when I was busy boating, there was an enormous gap in my life. I didn't know how long I was going to live, but it seemed that the doctor's initial predictions had been wrong, for I was still here. If I was going to live, then I needed someone to share with, to love and be loved by. Cookie was wonderful but a bit short on conversation. I had to decide if I was going to carry on boating for ever or I was going to live a normal life - and hopefully meet someone to live it with me. It was a decision I'd never expected to have to make, because I'd already lived so much longer than anyone had predicted. I was, however, still on a heavy regime of drugs. The regular tests showed that things were fairly stable for now but the doctors told me outright that this would not continue and eventually the cancer would get me. The one thing they couldn't say was when. The big question in my mind was would it be fair to meet someone, only to die on them in the not too distant future.

I had a long chat with my sister Di about this conundrum. Her opinion was that as long as I was completely honest, then I could leave it to the other person to decide. She said, "You'll be fine; just go with it".

So I joined 'Soulmates', the Guardian newspaper's online dating service. I've always been pretty leftwing politically and the Guardian is a leftwing paper, so at least I stood a chance of meeting someone likeminded. I wasn't very good at selling myself but even so I met quite a few people through Soulmates. Only one woman ran off when I said that I was ill; the majority were fine with it. I wasn't actually expecting to find anybody special, but it got me out of the boat and meeting people, and that was the object of the exercise really. I genuinely thought that I was unlikely to meet anybody who would want any sort of long term relationship with me, given how ill I was, apart from all the usual difficulties of meeting someone compatible.

As time went by, I decided that my profile was awful. I thought, "Even Cookie could do better than that". This thought gave me an idea. I wrote a new profile, writing as though Cookie was writing it for me. It began, "I'm Cookie, David's fluffy white cat. He's useless at this, so I thought I'd have a go." Then it carried on in a similar vein. It seemed a bit trite, but I put a bit of humour in and I thought that maybe it would make me stand out more in the crowd. It turned out to be the best thing I ever did...

It wasn't Helen who wrote back to me - it was her cat Magnus! She'd read my profile supposedly written by Cookie, and been intrigued enough to reply, to Cookie, in the same way. She was single, a cat lover, and living near Ashbourne in Derbyshire.

She was a helicopter instructor and freelance writer, which was intriguing. She seemed like an interesting person. Right from the start it sounded promising. But the timing was dreadful. By then Easter was approaching, and I was leaving the marina about a week later. I'd decided that I was going boating again, at least for that year. I was going north, to York. That was as near as I could get to Josh, who was still at university in Scarborough. I had this idea that I could go on the train and see him, from York, and we could spend some time together. Everything a young lad at University wants of course – his dad just round the corner! But Josh and I did get on very well, so it seemed like a good idea at the time.

Meanwhile, Helen and I had exchanged a few emails, then started chatting on the phone. We seemed to get on really well. So I suggested we meet when I was a little closer to her, since I was heading north anyway, and I really didn't want to see her in a dismal place like Alvecote!

The Easter holidays started, I went up to Scarborough and fetched Josh, and I told him we were going back to York on the boat. It was the Easter break, so we only had a couple of weeks together, but I had worked out that we could do it. So we set off, and I arranged to meet Helen in Alrewas. It seemed a long way for her to travel from Ashbourne, but she said it was fine and not far at all. I remember that I was quite surprised, because when you're on a boat, it is indeed a long way. Alvecote to Alrewas took three days by water; it's about 25 minutes by car. Asbourne is another hour's drive, but if there was a canal - which there isn't - that would be another week. Distances appear much further when you do a lot of boating. Even though I was a motorist myself I regularly fell into this trap.

So Helen and I met, and we went to a local pub for lunch, and we got on really, really well. I thought that Helen was a really lovely cat-orientated person. She came back to *LadyRiverMouse* and met Cookie, and she loved her, which of course was important to me. She also met Josh, and later I asked him what he thought. He said, "She's nice", which is as good as you get out of Josh. I remember that I was completely mesmerised by Helen's big 'blingy' cat watch that she had at the time. I hadn't mentioned my illness yet in emails or on the phone because I felt that was something I needed to do face to face. But now I told her, and, most importantly, this didn't seem to faze her at all. I thought that this might really be the start of a promising relationship. But I had made plans, and I had Josh with me, and I had to get to York. So we tentatively arranged to meet later on, and left things like that.

Chapter 10
Yorkshire...as Far North as Possible

There was more to my decision to go to Yorkshire than just a desire to be near to Josh. I'd never boated on the wide and deep waterways of the North West. There's still lots of commercial traffic on them, and some of those are really big boats. There are tugs pulling lines of dumb barges (ones without engines which need to be towed) known as 'Tom Puddings' and even the occasional ship. These are exciting places for boating, and the real surprise is the lack of pleasure craft. It's often said that the waterways are becoming more and more crowded. In the honey pot locations like Braunston this is undeniably true, but in the wild open waters of Yorkshire you do well to spot another boat.

However, as I boated on over the next few weeks, I was thinking long and hard about my personal situation. It was early days yet of course, and we had only met the once, but I really felt that this thing with Helen might turn into a long term relationship. That would almost certainly mean that I'd have to give up boating. The alternative – that Helen could take to a waterways existence - never even crossed my mind. She had four cats for goodness sake! During this time I went really quiet and didn't talk to Helen that much. We sent each other some emails, but that was all. She said later that after a short time she'd assumed that I just wasn't interested in anything more than friendship and email correspondence. She even told her friends that she'd met a really nice guy, but he was off boating and didn't seem that keen on her. However, it never occurred to me to think about how she might perceive the situation, even though I didn't want to lose her. But then, I'm a man, and we don't dwell on things like that!

The trip to York turned out to be a lot more eventful than perhaps it should have been. I set off from Alrewas, heading up the Trent, a route I'd done before. But when I got to the junction with the Soar, instead of turning right as I had previously, I carried straight on towards Nottingham. We stopped in Nottingham for a day. We went on the Nottingham Wheel, which was a ferris wheel in the middle of the town, and we generally had a pleasant day in the town.

The next day we got to Newark, where we moored just below the castle. I went for a little walk, and decided to stop there for the night. I was sitting on deck watching the evening light fade over the Trent and admiring the age old arches of the stone bridge when another narrowboat came down the river. They were travelling quite quickly as there was a good flow on the river, and it surprised me when they tried to turn in front of the arches of the bridge. It would have been an ambitious move at any time, but with the river high and running fast it was hopeless. Needless to say they didn't make it and were swept sideways across the arches of the bridge. There was no immediate danger but their boat was stuck fast – pinned by the current. Suspecting that these folk were not expert boaters, I went to offer them a hand. Between us we got a rope to the bank and then I could slowly pull the boat off the bridge and get it free. It was quite a struggle, but eventually we got them to the bank, although they were still pointing downstream. So I showed them how to turn a boat by using a line ashore and the power of the current. I think I earned their gratitude.

However, that was only the first unexpected event of the trip. Later that night as we sat inside there was a little 'ping' on the roof of the boat, and then another, and another, like small missiles landing. Youths on the castle opposite were using us for target practice - throwing stones on to us! The normally placid Josh was having none of this; he can have quite a temper at times. He got up and chased the lads along the towpath. They saw that there was somebody coming – somebody young and quite large and strong looking - and disappeared pronto! Excitement over.

The next day we arrived at Cromwell lock, just north of Newark. Cromwell is the start of the tidal section of the Trent, which might seem surprising as it's such a long way from the sea. But the land is as flat as a pancake all the way from there to the east coast. You can actually go on the river all the way from Cromwell lock to Naburn in York without a single lock, but not in a narrowboat because you have to join the River Humber and it is too dangerous. The narrowboat route is to leave the Trent at Keadby for the South Yorkshire navigations – which are canals - rejoining the route at the River Ouse at Selby.

The tidal Trent from Cromwell to Keadby is still too far to do in one go. The lock keepers are very experienced and know the river well, so before leaving Cromwell I had a timetable to go with my charts of the river, and I knew that I would be expected at Keadby at the appropriate time. Going downstream on the four hours of a falling tide takes a narrowboat about halfway - to Torksey This is the start of the Fossdyke Navigation to Lincoln. There I was to stop for the night. I had been given given the time of midday to leave next day, when the tide would have turned and it would be falling again.

Despite the fact that the river overall was uncrowded, Torksey is a busy mooring spot. Moorings on tidal rivers are few and far between, and I had some difficulty in finding a space. I had to moor up against somebody else, and they moaned about it a bit. However, they were understanding when I explained that I'd be gone the next day.

From Cromwell to Torksey is quite civilised boating in most ways. It's fairly calm, but you need to follow a chart, because there are sandbanks and they shift. But that section is not too difficult. The section from Torksey down to Keadby is much more...shall we say 'interesting'. The currents are stronger, the sandbanks are deeper and they shift more quickly, and the tides are higher. As I went through Gainsborough, two small but powerful boats came the other way at speed. In Gainsborough the river goes through a section which has steel pilings on both sides, presumably to keep the water out of Gainsborough in case of flood. The wash of these boats hit these pilings and came back, multiplying into sizeable waves about three feet high. They came up to the windows on *LadyRiverMouse*, and came over the deck and sloshed over my feet. I could see in advance that it was going to happen but there was nothing I could do but I did have my camera handy and got a video of the experience. It was yet another exciting event on this trip.

As maybe you can tell, quite skilled boating was needed for this route. I wouldn't have wanted to do this sort of thing when I first started, but it was 2010, and by now I was quite experienced. Also, I had my VHF radio on all the time and I was listening to the other traffic, which helped quite a bit. But you do need some experience to tackle the tidal Trent, especially in a narrowboat. You're going down on a falling tide, and the banks are rushing by really quickly; well, quickly by narrowboat standards anyway.

Before long the M18 bridge came into view. I knew that Keadby lock was about half a mile beyond the bridge, so I gave the tiller to Josh, and told him to give me a call when we were under the bridge, and I was going down to make a cup of tea. I'd just filled the kettle when the engine alarm went off. Of course I rushed back up. There was steam coming out of the engine room, and the temperature gauge was off the top of the scale. I shouted to Josh to stop the engine, which he did. I opened the engine room hatch, and there was just a cloud of steam. We'd broken down, right in the middle of the tidal Trent!

Now, normally in these circumstances you would anchor to prevent the boat being swept along by the tide. However, it was just coming to slack water. There was no current on the river at all, no traffic, and no wind to blow us about. So although I told Josh to keep a lookout, I wasn't too worried. We were in the middle of the river, but there was no immediate problem; we weren't going anywhere. I told Josh to shout to me if a boat came along and we'd somehow get out of the way; then I set about repairing the engine. When the steam cleared it became clear that the problem was only a hose which had come off its fitting. It was the work of a couple of minutes - and some scalded fingers - to put it back and tighten it up.

However, I then had to refill the whole cooling system. You can't put cold water into a hot engine without doing serious damage so I needed some hot water. Fortunately we'd been boating for four hours by this time and the domestic water, heated by the engine, was nearly at boiling point. So all I had to do was fill the kettle from the hot tap in the kitchen and use that to fill the engine. But it took a long time; the engine held a lot of water, and I lost count of how many kettlefuls it took. Eventually I got it filled again and, with the engine restarted, the temperature gauge went back to normal – though there were a few anxious minutes before it did that.

As we carried cautiously on towards Keadby, I gave the lock keeper a call on the VHF radio to say that we were on our way. No answer. I tried again, and again there was no answer. Then I noticed that there was a mobile number for him. So I called it, and he answered, and in the background were definite 'in the pub' sounds. It turned out that there was a pub right next to the lock. Anyway, he said that he'd be there in ten minutes and have the gates open for us. So finally we got to Keadby lock, and I've never been so happy to get into a lock in my life. That breakdown in the middle of the tidal Trent was one of my scariest moments. That sort of thing was not supposed to happen, especially not with a new engine. Sadly it wasn't going to be the last time that the engine failed on me... But anyway, the next day was spent in the village of Keadby, looking for more antifreeze to top up the system.

We were now on the South Yorkshire Navigations. These are the canals which bypass the Humber Estuary. They go inland a little way, and are actually a mixture of canals and rivers. They run west, then turn north, then do a little bit of twiddling, as it were. They go across the River Humber upstream, where it's safe, and then join the Selby canal, which cuts off a corner. At last you end up in Selby, ready to go up to York on the tidal Ouse.

When we got to Selby we were as usual running late – at least, Josh was. It had been his Easter holidays, but term was about to start. So he went back to Scarborough by train, leaving me to boat from Selby to York on my own. Selby is well worth a visit at any time. There is a huge abbey, lively shops, and very friendly people. This is a place where if you stop to chat, complete strangers will share their life history, that of their friends and relatives, and anything else they can think of. There was no hurry now that Josh had gone back, so I stayed for a while. Eventually all good things come to an end and it was time to leave. I made an appointment with the lock keeper at Selby, to go out on to the Ouse early one morning, about 5.30 or 6.00 am, on the rising tide. I was going up to Naburn, the lock you come to a few miles before York.

There was a mist on the river that morning. There was nobody about, and it was as quiet and peaceful as you get. As I left the lock and turned upstream there was only the noise of the engine and that was muffled by the white envelope of mist. They were expecting me at Naburn lock, because they always know exactly what time you're going to arrive.

All these locks are manned, as is every tidal lock. Any route with large commercial traffic always has lock keepers, though not necessarily 24/7; sometimes the lock keepers only arrive just before the boats. In fact, if they're commercial boats the lock keeper will arrive in a van about 10 minutes before the boat is due and then just leave, because everything is timetabled.

I stayed for a little while at Naburn lock, but it's in the middle of nowhere really. So soon I was driven by empty cupboards to York itself, where there are shops and facilities. I moored just under Lendal bridge by the beautifully kept Museum Gardens, just above the spot the trip boats depart from, and I stayed there for a couple of weeks. I walked round the city walls, I visited the National Railway Museum, and I did all the other normal tourist things. York is everything that the tourist guides promise - but I did encounter one problem. You can't buy a loaf of bread in York. You can buy a designer sandwich, or a slice of delicious cake, but you try buying a loaf of bread; it's really, really difficult. Almost all the shops are aimed at the visiting tourists. There is a market, for fruit and vegetables and meat and fish, but no bread stall. The only place I found selling bread was the famous Betty's Teashop. In addition to tea and cakes they will sell you a loaf, but at a price about three times that of a normal shop. Delicious bread though! But to be fair, I lived quite well in York.

I wanted to go to Ripon next, because that's as far north as you can travel on the inland waterways system. On the way I stopped at Boroughbridge, which was a lovely sleepy place, with a very well stocked delicatessen in which I spent far too much money. Then I went on to Ripon. In Ripon you have to be really, really careful not to overstay. Like everywhere else on the system there are mooring restrictions, but in Ripon there's a member of the public who takes boat numbers and reports you if you're a second over your due date. It seems as though they don't want boats to come under their particular flat window, so they make it as hard as possible for boaters, and they make sure they don't have them mooring there for a moment longer than they absolutely have to. It's well known among boaters that you don't overstay in Ripon. The strange thing is that just outside the basin, by the lock, you can moor forever and nobody will bother you. Anyway, in Ripon I collected a little plaque which said I'd reached the head of the Navigation, which I still have. And then I did the only thing possible; I turned round and headed south again.

Chapter 11
Yorkshire...Plans to Give up Boating

As I was heading back down the river Ouse towards York, there was a shout from the bank, a really panicky shout: "Please help". There were a couple on the bank, but the woman was stuck in soft ground close to the river edge. It seemed my eventful boating was to continue. I nosed *LadyRiverMouse* as close as I could into the bank, but banks shelve, and there was a lot of mud, so I couldn't get very near. The man asked me if I had a rope, and I said, "I think you're going to need more than just a rope". But I passed him a length of rope, and I also passed the gangplank from off the roof. Then I tied the boat to a tree as close to them as I could get. I couldn't get off the boat to help, but at least I could throw things across the gap and offer advice and support. The man put the plank down and put the rope under his partner's shoulders, and he pulled and she pushed, and between them they got her out. But it was a struggle, and I was on the point of phoning for the emergency services. In fact I wanted to phone the emergency services anyway, but they asked me not to. But at one point I thought that I'd give it another five minutes and then I'd get on the phone anyway, because things were getting silly and I wasn't going to sit there and watch someone drown. She came out plastered in mud, and he was not too happy with her for getting stuck in the first place. At that point I left them to it. So that was another David rescue; I was beginning to feel as though I was making a habit of getting people out of scrapes, on this trip. But it was only the next day when someone returned the favour...

Linton Lock was my last of the day and I was probably tired, which may account for the predicament I found myself in. I had let *LadyRiverMouse* down in the lock and somehow dropped the rope so that she was floating around nowhere near the ladder and I had no way of getting back on board. I was contemplating my predicament and was even considering refilling the lock. But this would have to be done very carefully, as I would have no control over the boat. As I stood there, somewhat perplexed, a young lad, laden with supermarket bags, came wandering along the towpath. He took one look; dropped his shopping and swung down the ladder like a monkey on a stick. With a seemingly impossible leap, he was on *LadyRiverMouse's* deck, and a few minutes later he had driven her out of the lock and safely on to the lock mooring. I never even had time to thank him. He just picked up his shopping and carried on. There are some good people in the world.

After that I went back down to York, where I stopped off again because I liked it so much. Then it was down to Naburn again. As I was in Naburn lock going down, with the lock keeper letting the water out, I became aware of something in the lock with me - not a boat, but something alive. I looked down, and a head poked out of the water. It was a seal. I couldn't believe I'd find a seal this far from the coast, but there it was. Anyway, it followed me all the way down to Selby. It would swim along, and every so often it would poke its head out and have a look at me, then swim a bit further. I believe the locals called him Sammy; they knew him well. But seeing him was very special for me.

By the time I got to Selby there was quite a current flowing, and I had to do a bit of nifty manoeuvring to get into Selby lock. I had to go down past the lock, turn around, and come back upstream under power to get into the lock. The lock keeper didn't think I was going to make it. I talked to him afterwards and he said that he didn't think I'd have enough power to get upstream against the current. But with my new bigger engine, I knew that I could. Then it was back to Selby, where I spent quite some time. I collected my car, and found that I could park it in a lay-by right next to the boat, which was very handy. Once again I enjoyed the friendliness of the local folk. This was the real Yorkshire. However, it was at Selby that I dropped my mobile phone in the canal, where it probably still lies. I tried unsuccessfully to retrieve it with a landing net, but then someone stole the net while it was drying on the roof. There are always exceptions to generalisations about people, even in Yorkshire. But mostly I thoroughly enjoyed my stay in Selby.

It was at Selby, however, that things really changed for me in a much deeper sense. Firstly, everything seemed to be going so well that I decided I didn't need my antidepressants any more. So I stopped taking them, which turned out to be a mistake. I got very miserable, and then I began to think about Helen. I wanted to contact her, but I couldn't; she was on holiday in Scotland with no email access. I couldn't even phone her, as my mobile was at the bottom of the canal. Anyway, I decided then that despite being enjoyable, this boating way of life was ultimately pointless. I realised that I needed to do something with my life other than aimless trugging round the waterways system. Basically, I felt that I definitely needed someone to share my life with, and sooner rather than later. This incident was probably the catalyst for my decision to give up boating and develop my relationship with Helen, if she wanted to of course. I still didn't know how she felt about me.

I decided then and there that I'd leave Yorkshire. I hung around in Selby just a little longer, until Josh's term finished, as I knew I'd need his help for the next section – going through the Huddersfield narrow canal and Standedge tunnel. My original plan had been to go over the Leeds/Liverpool, but I had to cancel that as there wasn't enough water in that part of the canal system; this was summer 2010, and there was a nationwide drought. That left me with only one route across the Pennines through Huddersfield. Then would come a long trip through the North West, ending up in Leek, the closest point to Helen's home on the canal system. Then I could begin to see more of her. Of course, I hadn't yet told her of these plans.

One of the things about narrowboats is the lack of storage. This is particularly a problem when your son is vacating his university accommodation for the summer and needs somewhere to store his stuff; even more so when he is studying music and that includes an electric piano, a huge amplifier and several guitars - not to mention the saxophone. The nearest storage unit I could arrange was in York and it took three trips. But I did allow two guitars and the saxophone on board.

On the day I left Selby with Josh the sky turned red and it rained. I felt as though it was crying for me, as I really did love Yorkshire. I left the county with very mixed feelings; very sad, but knowing in my heart that it was time to move on. I was heading for other things, and possibly even a new way of life. But firstly, I was heading for Huddersfield.

On this trip Cookie brought in her one and only live catch ever. It was a shrew which we called Mortimer. Cookie brought him on board and let him go, and Mortimer lived on board for two nights and nearly three days. He lodged behind the bookcase next to Cookie's food and would come out and eat her food and drink her water, then disappear behind the bookcase again. Then at night Mortimer would run around all over the boat and over our beds, and we would try and catch him under a saucepan so that we could free him on the bank. But he was too quick for us and managed to get away, even from under a saucepan; I still don't know how he did that. However, on the third morning Josh said that we didn't have to look for him any more, as he was dead on Josh's bed. I suspect that Cookie finally caught her prey but a shrew's somewhat ineffective means of defence is that they taste awful, so he remained uneaten. We tossed him unceremoniously into the hedge and carried on. What else could we do?

We boated through Wakefield, which is the most soulless place in the whole world. It's dismal, with dusty streets, traffic, and not much else. Any thoughts of staying in there evaporated after about the first 30 seconds. And so we came to Huddersfield, which is a complete contrast. It's the original home of

Harold Wilson, and they celebrate this fact with a big statue of him outside the railway station. There's also a lovely fountain and some splendid architecture. I liked Huddersfield.

While I was stopped in Huddersfield I finally got round to visiting Helen again. There's a bit of a story behind this... My car was being looked after by a friend, Sara, whom I'd got to know through Soulmates about three months before Helen first wrote to me. Sara and I had written to each other a lot and we'd become friends, although it was obvious to both of us that our friendship was never going to develop into anything more. She was a dog person, for a start! However, she knew all about Helen and how I was feeling. When I arrived in Huddersfield, I decided to go and collect the car, and Sara asked me if I'd been to see Helen yet, as she had several times before that. She seemed much more concerned about my procrastination than I was! Women understand these things. Finally I got the point...

So the day after I picked up my car I drove down to see Helen. I was looking forward to seeing her again, and I was also intrigued by the fact that she had a new Maine Coon kitten, Xena. This little nine week old scrap of fur had cost her several hundred pounds, and I was curious about a kitten that cost that much money. My previous experience of kittens was that they were free! I also took a bag of dirty washing. I used to do that to all my friends; I'd either turn up with a towel over my arm and ask to use the bath, or a bag of dirty washing and ask if I could use the washing machine. It took me a lot longer to drive down than I expected because I took the direct (and more scenic) route over the Pennines; for the way back Helen showed me the route via the M1, which is longer but much faster.

Anyway, it worked out really well. Xena the new kitten was gorgeous, and all the other pussycats were lovely; there were five of them now, and I even got a glimpse of Aslan, the shy one. They lived in a beautifully situated house in a village in the Pennines, but I thought it needed some upkeep. I opened the rickety gate and found myself wondering if I'd eventually end up changing it. I stayed for the afternoon; then I had to get back. But after that visit Helen and I started phoning each other regularly, every day in fact, and sometimes several times a day. And meanwhile I boated the Huddersfield narrow canal with Josh – or the Huddersfield narrow mud, as I called it, because there was hardly any water and it was really hard work.

It was on this canal that I nearly lost the boat! We were travelling up through the locks, and there was very little water, but I judged that there was just enough to get us through the next section. I went into the lock, filled it, opened the gates, and drove the boat out. What I didn't know was that there was a leak in the lock which was so bad that the water level was dropping as I was leaving. *LadyRiverMouse* grounded on the top cill, and the back of the boat started to drop down; the weight of the engine carrying her down at the back. This happened quite slowly but there was nothing I could do. I sent Josh up to the next lock to run more water down but the next section was bone dry. In desperation I phoned British Waterways, and they said they'd get somebody out to me the next day. I said that might be too late, and I was wondering who else I could call when finally the boat slid off the cill. Suddenly 13 tons of boat was rushing backwards towards the rather flimsy gates at the bottom of the lock. I just had a brief vision of *LadyRiverMouse* going straight through and the thought that I was going to completely destroy the Huddersfield narrow canal, when instinct took over. I jumped back on board and hit the throttle full ahead. The thrashing propeller stopped *LadyRiverMouse* just short of the gates. We spent the night in the lock; we couldn't do anything else. There was no water; it had all drained away. The British Waterways guys turned up in the morning.

That was actually the most terrifying moment in my whole five years of boating. It wasn't until afterwards that it all hit me, and I found myself shaking. I had been worried stiff about Cookie, but she seemed to have been asleep during the whole drama and not bothered in the slightest. The problem was that the whole canal was drying up. The British Waterways guys got us up in the end by flushing water down from the reservoir at the top of all the locks, but it was very slow and difficult. I felt that we'd pulled the boat all the way up through mud.

Chapter 12
Lancashire and Cheshire

At the top of the locks was the prize – Standedge Tunnel. At three miles, it's the longest tunnel on the system. You might wonder why I considered it a 'prize' when I've said before that I hated tunnels, but this tunnel is different. This tunnel is an event. A British Waterways pilot comes through it with you on your boat, they only take three boats a day, and only twice a week, so you have to book your passage. There's a service tunnel running alongside which used to be a railway tunnel, and it's linked to the canal tunnel by cross adits (small passages linking two tunnels) at intervals. As you pass through the tunnel a British Waterways man in a van goes through this service tunnel and appears in the adits checking on progress and ensuring that all is well. There's a real live railway tunnel as well on the other side, again with cross adits, and sometimes you can see the lights of the trains going by. At one point you enter a cavern which is like a huge cathedral, with stalactites hanging down. And at other times it's so tight that you can barely fit the boat through. Some boaters won't go through because its been known to damage boats, but the whole journey was totally fascinating and I wouldn't have missed it for the world.

When we got to the other side of the tunnel,

the Lancashire side, it started raining. This was the end of the long drought, although of course I didn't know that at the time. It rained and rained and rained; we came down the Lancashire side of the Huddersfield narrow canal in a cascade of water. It was running over the weirs and over the lock gates, and over our clothes. Everything was soaked. The difference between the two sides couldn't have been more marked.

We stopped at the first little town, and – making up for lost time, as it were - I went to see Helen again, this time taking Josh too. I asked him if he wanted to see Helen's new kitten and of course he did. Helen and Josh seemed to get on well, as they had the first time they met back in Alrewas, and I was pleased about that. And she and I couldn't stop talking to each other, which is always a good sign.

Then more boating...first came Stockport, then Whaley Bridge. Next I turned on to the Macclesfield canal and went down to Congleton. This would eventually take me back on to the Trent and Mersey, then to the Caldon canal and on to Leek. However, as we were coming down the Marple flight, an oil leak, which had been present as a small drip for a few days, started to become an absolute flood. By the time I got to the bottom of the locks all the oil had drained out of the hydraulic gearbox and I had no drive. By pouring oil in, I just managed to get as far as the next main road bridge, from where I phoned Penkridge Boat Services, as the engine was still under guarantee. I told them my gearbox had failed; all the oil had drained out. They said they'd send out an engineer. The chap they sent was a very experienced guy called Jim from Stockport. He climbed down into my engine room with his toolbox and a bag of spare parts, but this fault was beyond fixing by the canal side. In the end he said he'd take away the faulty part to his workshop and do it there. So he did that, but of course it left me without an engine. This is disastrous on a narrowboat, even if you're not moving. I couldn't run the engine for anything; I couldn't charge the batteries, I couldn't get hot water, and it would be two or three days before he came back!

At this point Helen quite literally came to my rescue. I told her the whole story next time we spoke on the phone, and she offered to help. She drove all the way over to Congleton, which is quite a long way from Ashbourne; she picked us up and drove us to Morrisons in Congleton, so that we could buy some supplies. I decided this woman was really, really special if she would do that when she still hardly knew me. Now I really had to go to Leek, spend some time there, and see more of her.

Jim came back exactly when he'd said he would, which surprised me a little, because as I said before narrowboat time can be a bit flexible. It turned out that the part had been incorrectly assembled in the factory, in such a way that there was nothing to hold the oil seal in. Over time it had just worked loose and all the oil had come out. I was lucky that I'd used the boat as much as I had, because if I'd just used her on holiday trips, then it would have lasted years and been out of guarantee by the time it went wrong. As it was I didn't have to pay anything. Jim put it back together again and we were ready to go, except that I had a bilge full of oil, which took me ages to clear out. At first I didn't know what to do with it, but later on I found a boatyard in Stoke-on-Trent with an oil disposal place, and I was able to scoop all the oil out with a modified milk container which I cut to shape.

Soon after this an incident occurred which showed me just how important it is to be constantly aware when boating. We were going up the last lock of the day on the Caldon Canal and looking forward to our evening meal in Endon, on the outskirts of Stoke-on-Trent. Josh opened the lock gates and I drove *LadyRiverMouse* into the chamber, as we had done so many times before. Then I closed the gates while Josh went forward to open the paddles and let the water in. However, on this occasion my attention was drawn to something in the cabin, and I stood on the top step to have a closer look. Josh raised the paddles rather suddenly and *LadyRiverMouse* surged forwards against the gate. It wasn't much of a collision but it was enough. I somersaulted off the step and pitched headlong into the cabin. As I fell I put out an arm to save myself and my thumb caught on the side of the bunk. The pain was immediate and intense and I could see at a glance that the thumb was at a strange angle. There was little we could do straight away, so I bandaged it as best I could and we continued to the visitor mooring at Endon.

Later that evening I realised that things were not going well – the pain was worse and the whole hand was swelling up nastily. I had no idea where the nearest hospital was; in fact, in relation to the world of roads and vehicles I had no idea where I was anyway. So I reached for my mobile phone and called for an ambulance. A paramedic in a 4 x 4 arrived quickly and ran through a whole gamut of tests - including an ECG - and pronounced me fairly well but with a very sore thumb. He added that it really needed to be x-rayed, and after a moment or two of discussion with his control office, he offered to drive me to the nearest hospital. Silly me - I thought that's what ambulances did all the time, but not in Stoke on Trent apparently without calling in first.

I was dropped off at a small hospital somewhere on the outskirts of the city. To this day I don't know where it was. After a short wait I was seen and told again that I needed an x-ray. The problem was that their x-ray department was closed for the night. I would need to get to the main hospital's accident and emergency department somewhere in the vast metropolis of Stoke. The only help they could give me was the telephone number of a local taxi firm. But this was enough and about half an hour later I was outside the city's main A & E.

Inside the place was grim in the extreme. There were people everywhere. It was a normal weekday evening but it seemed to me that most of the patients were intoxicated in some way. Some of them were lying on the floor and looked to be on something far from legal. I registered at a little window and, given the crowds, was somewhat surprised to hear my name called a couple of minutes later. This was just an initial assessment and the nurse asked me to go over the whole story from the beginning, and also asked if I had taken any pain killers. One of the benefits of being a cancer patient is that you are not short of pain relief. I reeled off a list of various drugs, some of which are prescription only, and most of which should not be taken together, to increasingly raised eyebrows. Eventually it was decided that I didn't need any more pain relief, but yet again I was told that I did need an x-ray. I was directed to a small waiting room pleasantly free of drunks and junkies.

After an hour or so I was called and my wrist was finally x-rayed. I remember this as the most painful bit of the whole night. I had to get my hand flat on the table, which was not the way it wanted to be. It was then another hour or so until I was seen with the results. I was lucky; no broken bones, just torn ligaments - but they wanted to plaster my arm, "just in case", as they put it. Another waiting room, another queue. By this time it was well into the early hours of the morning, and as I watched the endless procession of plastered folk (all meanings of the word) coming out of the little cubicles, I had a desperate desire to be home. I didn't want my arm in plaster "just in case"; what I wanted was my cat. I went for a walk to get my thoughts together, past the crowd of smokers in a fug on the doorstep. There, as though waiting for me, was a glistening white taxi...

I was home in about 20 minutes and a little later my mobile rang. The hospital number showed in the display. They were probably missing me. I switched it off.

This story has a little more to it. Three weeks later, when I was in my GP's surgery for a regular check up, my doctor asked who'd removed my cast. It had gone on my record as having been done and he was just wondering. I wondered who they plastered that night that wasn't me!

Finally we boated into Leek. As we did so, Josh stood on the roof of *LadyRiverMouse* and serenaded the local wildlife and dog walkers with a medley of tunes on the saxophone. He would give this sort of impromptu concert from time to time, and we only ever had smiles and applause from the people we saw.

Leek is not really much of a canal terminus. There are no buildings or facilities, but we tied up there anyway because that is where I wanted to be for a while. It was September 2010.

Chapter 13
Winter on the Caldon Canal

Most canals end in a wharf, with a proper place to moor and a few buildings. There is somewhere to get water and dispose of rubbish, maybe a shop, and most probably a pub. The end of the Leek branch of the Caldon canal has nothing at all like this. There is not even a proper 'winding hole' (turning point – wind pronounced as in the stuff that blows and not what you do to a clock) for a boat of *LadyRiverMouse*'s 50 feet. You have to reverse back a couple of hundred yards to a suitable spot. The canal just peters out by the side of an enormous scrapyard. The feeder to Rudyard Lake carries on enticingly through a country park, but is only a few inches deep. A footpath traces a route between the heaps of scrap metal and a dusty concrete works into the industrial estate which has covered the last half mile or so of the original canal, isolating the town of Leek from its waterway and the canal from any meaningful facilities.

All of this means that boats arrive, take a look, and depart. This is a shame because Leek has all the shops you could wish for plus a lively market and a thriving community. It is possible to walk to Morrisons supermarket, which is just beyond the industrial estate, but it's a long way to carry heavy bags of shopping. It helped that I had a shopping trolley, a neat little contraption that folded up into something handbag-sized for storage on the boat. But it was a very long walk into the centre of town.

In spite of all this, or perhaps because of it, the Leek terminus is a beautiful and tranquil place. But I found myself the only boat there on several occasions. The nearest boating facilities were at Endon, a few miles back towards Stoke on Trent. There I could find a sanitary station with the all-important pump out machine for the effluent tank, a water point from which to fill the water tank, and all the rest of the things you need for everyday life. There was a small shop and post office and even a chemist.

There are, however, no refuelling facilities anywhere on the Caldon Canal, which is what this is. So I used to buy diesel in small amounts at local garages. Fortunately in the Leek area it was easy to find garages selling red diesel, which is untaxed and therefore cheaper, and can be used for off-road vehicles such as tractors, boats and so on. Technically tax is due on diesel used to move a boat, but not on that used for domestic things like generating electricity and heating water. When you fill up at a boatyard there is a calculation to be done on how much diesel is actually taxed. It's all very complicated. Local garages had never heard of all this, so to stay within the law I would occasionally buy some ordinary 'white' diesel and add that to the tank, keeping a record in a little notebook in case I was asked. I never was.

The canal to Leek is really only a side branch of the main Caldon Canal which in fact carries on to Froghall. Both branches are spectacularly beautiful as they twist and turn through narrow valleys but, similarly to Leek, the Froghall terminus has little to recommend it. I promised Josh a meal in the pub there but a twenty minute walk only led us to a boarded up building. In fairness I didn't get to the wharf proper as that was through a very low tunnel - unbelievably low in fact. I did try, but even with everything stripped off the roof *LadyRiverMouse* stubbornly remained a couple of centimetres too tall.

I'd given up any plans for long distance boating at that stage, at least for the winter. After that...I didn't know. It depended a lot on how things went in my relationship with Helen. The university term was due to start, and Josh went back for his final year of studying. I wanted to stay in the Leek area for the winter, partly because it was a nice place, and I couldn't face another winter in a marina, not after the last one. It was also fairly vandal free – always a consideration on any canal. But my main reason – and the most important one - for staying there was that it was near to Helen, as near as I could get on the canal system.

Helen came to see me while I was moored in Leek, and I went to see her. She came to the boat, and she met me in Morrisons cafe, and also at The Hollybush, a popular canalside pub between Endon and Leek. We also met for lunch at a pub in Waterhouses, a village about halfway between Ashbourne and Leek. In fact, we finally began to see each other fairly regularly and get to know each other properly. I started to go over to Helen's house for the odd day, we went out together to various events, and she introduced me to the local animal rescue organisation where she was a volunteer cat socialiser. Meanwhile I chugged back and forth between Leek and Endon at intervals, so as to stay legal, although I never saw any mooring wardens, and I was never challenged or anything during that time.

However, it was a very hard winter. Helen went on holiday in November, on a group snorkelling trip to the Maldives which she had organised some months earlier. Her regular cat sitter, Maureen, arrived from London to care for the cats, and I offered to be a back-up if needed. But it was not to be. Just about the time that Helen left, I had moored the boat in Endon, and arranged to take Cookie to stay with my mum for a few days, while I visited Lizzie, who was now living in Ireland. I was planning to drive to Fishguard, then catch the ferry to Ireland and drive to Waterford, where Lizzie was living. I was a bit worried about this trip anyway, as it meant leaving the boat in Endon by the side of the canal. Although Endon is a pretty safe place, I was somewhat doubtful about it; but it was better than Leek as there were other boaters there whom I could ask to keep an eye on things for me.

On the morning of my proposed trip I got up bright and early, and the whole world had turned into an ice cube! It was really, really cold, minus sixteen degrees. I didn't know that then, but it was the start of a fortnight long cold snap. I decided that I'd have to leave the heating on in the boat. So I put it on low, and I told the people on the boat next door that I'd done that, to keep the boat free of ice. But I was now even more worried about this trip. Nevertheless, I loaded Cookie and my suitcase into the car and started to defrost the windows. But as I turned the windscreen wipers on they went "Wheeeee...CLUNK", and stopped. I'd had trouble with these windscreen wipers before and the RAC had mended them once, but this looked terminal.

There was no way I could drive all the way to Ireland without windscreen wipers. However, I had plenty of time as the ferry crossing wasn't until next day. So I put Cookie and my suitcase back into the boat and took the car down to the local garage to see what they could do about my non-wiping wipers. They took one look and said, "It'll need a new windscreen wiper motor – the good news is that we can get one; bring it back later". That seemed OK, and I started to drive back to the boat.

On the way back there was a humpbacked bridge with traffic light controls on it. I stopped at the red, waited for the lights to change, selected first gear, took my foot off the clutch. There was a loud bang and the car dropped backwards. It clearly wasn't going anywhere. I phoned the garage which I'd just left and said, "Can you come and tow me in please". "What, with broken windscreen wipers?" they said, sounding puzzled. "Ah...", I replied. Then I took a deep breath and explained the situation.

So they came out with a tow truck, and diagnosed a broken driveshaft where it goes into the gearbox. Basically the gearbox was completely shot and so was the driveshaft. I was really glad that it happened there and not on the ferry to Ireland. I think someone was trying to tell me something.

Anyway, I cancelled my overnight accommodation and ferry crossing and phoned Lizzie with my apologies. I did eventually get to see her but not by car – I took the soft option and flew from Birmingham a few weeks later. For the time being I was going to stay in Endon. Actually I didn't have any choice; with my car towed away and *LadyRiverMouse* embedded in several inches of ice. The immediate problem was that I didn't have enough coal to keep the stove going. I'd assumed that I wasn't going anywhere by boat and I had let the stocks dwindle. I'd had the car to go and get coal, so it wasn't a problem. I tried the local Endon shops but this was a modern village and the houses didn't use solid fuel. The nearest supplier I could find was back in Leek.

So I took my little shopping trolley and I caught a bus. I got off the bus at Morrisons where I knew the filling station sold coal and I filled my trolley with as many sacks as I thought it could carry. As I lugged this shopping trolley back on to the bus I covered over the coal, as I had a feeling that some regulation somewhere said that you're not allowed to carry coal on a bus. I wasn't sure about that; it's certainly the case with gas. My poor shopping trolley just about made the trip, but it was never the same again; poor little thing; its wheels were all splayed out and it looked really tired – but I got my coal. At least I'd be warm.

To begin with it was really miserable, Helen was on holiday, it was freezing cold, and I couldn't go anywhere – even the buses were having trouble with the snow and ice. I knew I wouldn't be able to help with Helen's cats, but I hoped I wouldn't need to. I thought I'd check, so I phoned Maureen. I said, "I'm stuck here, the canal's frozen solid and the boat's iced in, and I've got no transport or anything; are you OK?" She replied, "There's 18 inches of snow here; I can't get out either". So it was just a matter of both of us buckling down. I was glad that I was in Endon with its local shop; if I'd have been in Leek I would have struggled even more. As it was I had to resort to my emergency toilet - a camping loo which I carried in case my usual toilet tank got full and I couldn't empty it. This loo had a cassette you removed and could carry to the emptying point. You can carry a cassette a fair way, but you can't carry a boat an inch. One of my very early lessons in boating was to always have a back up plan.

Eventually of course I got the car back, with a new gearbox. It was going again just about as Helen arrived back. The weather changed, and things started to thaw, and everything began to get much better.

Around this time Cookie had to have her teeth done. I'd noticed that she was dribbling, and I thought I'd better take her to a vet. I took her to a local practice in Endon, who diagnosed bad teeth. She needed to have an operation to have some teeth removed. It was a bit of a worry, especially as she was quite an old cat by now. Many old cats look thin and frail, but Cookie didn't, in spite of her diet; there was still plenty of her. I remember that the vet lifted her out of her basket with the words, "Is she losing weight?". Then he felt her and said, "No, she isn't is she?" And that vet had never seen her before! Bad teeth hadn't stopped her eating.

The weather got a lot worse later on in the winter, and we had several more cold snaps. During one of these, in early December, with the boat iced in and ice even on the inside of the windows, my hot water system broke down. This meant I couldn't even have a shower. At this point Helen came to my rescue as I was telling her my woes over the phone. "Oh, for goodness sake!" she said. "Bring Cookie and come and stay here, at least for a few days. I've got a spare room". So I did. I really liked the idea of being warm, and it would of course give me a chance to see if we should develop our relationship further.

But first things first – it meant I could have a bath, and wash my clothes, and get warm – all the things which house dwellers take for granted.

However, I was also worried about leaving the boat because things can freeze up - and in actual fact things did freeze up. A pipe burst, and unknown to me it started to drip into the bilges of the boat. This didn't become apparent till the Spring, when I was leaving the boat one day to go and see Helen The bilge alarm went off, showing that there was water in the bilges. This leaking pipe had slowly filled the boat with water. I panicked at first as I thought *LadyRiverMouse* was sinking but a call to my friendly narrowboat engineer sent me looking for dripping pipes. Almost always water in a narrowboat bilge has come from a domestic pipe leak. Eventually I found it behind one of the kitchen cupboards. It was only a tiny weep but enough to accumulate over several weeks. Tightening the joint fixed it quickly - it took a lot longer to pump and sponge the water from the bilge through the tiny access hatch.

But to get back to that December... I went over to Helen's and I stayed for a few days. I stayed in the spare room as Helen had suggested – although that arrangement was to change not too long afterwards. However, at this point our relationship was still much too new to even think about living together. I think Cookie liked it; she liked the warmth and the fact the house didn't move. As I said, she was getting old by now, she was about 12 or 13.

After that I started staying with Helen more often. Usually I'd come for the day, and more and more often I'd stay overnight. I never stayed for long, because I really didn't like leaving the boat alone for too long. And if I stayed for the night I'd always bring Cookie; I never left her alone on the boat overnight. That was a rule I had – if I stayed away I always took Cookie with me.

I should mention Helen's cats at this point. There were five of them: Gizmo the elderly woolly Persian (my favourite); Macavity (Cavi), the one-eyed ginger cat; Magnus, the prize winning Maine Coon; Aslan, a huge ginger chap whose size was only matched by his shyness; and Xena the pretty tortoiseshell Maine Coon kitten, now growing very large. To begin with I couldn't remember all of them and their names, but my love of cats would soon sort that out. For Cookie however this situation would prove to be quite a challenge.

Cookie had always been an only cat, and I wasn't sure how she'd get on with other cats. So we kept her separately in the spare room, and at this point she didn't really meet the resident cats. She had her own litter tray and feeding station, so she felt safe and didn't need to interact with the others if she didn't want to. She did indeed tend to keep apart from the other cats, even if she saw them. Several years later, she still lives mainly in the spare room and has her food there, although she does explore the rest of the house occasionally now, mainly to see what food the others have got. And she relates fairly well to Magnus, who is very gentle with her and seems to like her, if only for her 'senior' food which he seems to find irresistible.

We carried on in this way until Spring. When it finally thawed I moved the boat. However, I did this a little too early. It hadn't thawed as thoroughly as I thought it had, and I got stuck in the ice again between Endon and Leek. I had to go charging through it, effectively turning '*Mouse*' into an icebreaker! It was a hard winter, that one, but by Easter the canals had completely thawed and green shoots were heralding the onset of spring.

LadyRiverMouse in the snow

Chapter 14
Summer in Ashbourne

Despite it now being possible, I had definitely decided that I would do no more long distance boating. My aims in life had changed. Even apart from the relationship with Helen, which seemed to be going well, I realised that I'd actually had enough of boating. Remember, I'd never expected to do more than two years when I began as I hadn't expected to live this long. Now I'd spent more than four years cruising the waterways. My enthusiasm for it had largely gone. Instead of waking up and thinking, "Great, I'm going boating today", it had turned into: "Oh no, I've got to get up and move the boat and empty the loo and everything..." I'd had my fill of it. On one level I still enjoyed it all because I never stopped liking the wildlife and the water and the peace and quiet and the scenery – even if it was sometimes the backs of houses and factories. That was an element that was always good. But the actual boating itself had become a bit much, something of a chore, and I'd had enough; worked it out of my system as it were. So I really met Helen at about the optimum time, for me.

It turned out to be just the right time for her too. One of the first things I had known about Helen was that she worked as a pilot; specifically teaching people to fly helicopters. Later I discovered that she also wrote books and magazine articles about flying; work which meant long and irregular hours, travelling a lot, and meeting many people. It was a fascinating and varied life but for various reasons the emphasis was changing and she was now doing less and less flying and travelling, and spending more and more time at home writing. This meant she was feeling rather isolated, as her home was in a very rural area. It also meant that her priorities in life were changing. Basically she too now wanted someone to share her life with.

So I spent that Spring and early summer gradually moving in with Helen. It happened quite naturally; I simply went back to the boat less and less. We just enjoyed being together. I found plenty to do, fixing up things around the house and garden, including replacing the garden gate I'd thought about when I first visited...that seemed so long ago now. Helen was still doing quite a lot of aviation writing for books, magazines and websites, so she was actually quite busy much of the time. Her house was fairly large, especially by boating standards, and the garden even larger, and it had clearly been hard for her to keep up with all the domestic chores as well as her career. So now, while she worked, I did the housework and gradually repaired things, work I really enjoyed doing.

We also took a number of day trips to places in the Peak District, with Helen showing me her favourite haunts – Ilam, Buxton, Chatsworth, Eyam and many others. Things just seemed to work out naturally, and it felt like an easy, comfortable way of life, far more so than either of us would have expected quite so early on. She offered to take me helicopter flying, but somehow that never happened, as now she had less access to aircraft than when she had worked regularly as an instructor.

However, I went back to the boat at least once or twice a week, as I simply wouldn't leave it unattended by the side of the canal. And I still had most of my possessions there. I was living between the two places. Helen and I never really decided to live together; it just happened. In fact, my old friend Sara wrote and asked how I was getting on with Helen, and my reply was, "I don't really know, but we're having good fun finding out". I was happy, and that was enough. And, don't forget, I still thought I wasn't going to live for long. Long term decisions about my life didn't seem necessary. I did wonder how Helen felt about me being terminally ill, as she never mentioned it after I initially told her about it. Some time afterwards she said that she was very happy being with me, so she'd just decided to carry on and see what happened. "After all", she commented, "None of us really know how long we've got left, do we?"

Despite having tried most activities, Helen had never done any narrowboating. She wanted to try it, and that Spring I had just the thing for her. For at the end of April was the Royal Wedding. I'm a Republican and I definitely didn't want to see it, and Helen wasn't very interested in all the hype either. So we decided to escape it altogether by going off boating for a couple of days, and I picked a quiet route where there wasn't even likely to be TV reception. Helen found a cat sitter for her cats, and we took Cookie with us. I arranged that Helen would join me on the boat in Leek, and I had this little trip planned. It involved a bit of boating, three locks, a bit more boating, a couple more locks, an overnight stop in a beautiful but isolated area, and then the same trip back.

For me and Josh, the trip would have been no problem; in fact it would have been easy. But for me and Helen, with Helen not being a boating person and never having done any before, it was actually a great deal of work. She struggled at first to steer the boat, eventually commenting that manoeuvring it was a bit like hovering a helicopter, and that being a pilot definitely helped. But she did find it tricky initially, and it reminded me that most people do find it difficult when they first get on a boat. She worked the first lock, but found it hard work physically and got covered in oil, and after that she decided she preferred managing the boat in the lock (again saying that it was like manoeuvring a helicopter) while I did the actual opening and closing of the gates. That was no problem and worked well, and by the end of the first day she'd pretty much got the hang of it, though she did confess to me that while she enjoyed it, it really wasn't her thing. That was no problem, as we didn't need to go boating together. Actually, without realising, I'd thrown her very much in the deep end, as the first few bridges near Leek are very tight to get through, definitely not for beginners.

The route we took was from Leek to the junction with the main Caldon canal, through three locks, to a lunch stop at a pub. We then boated on through Cheddleton, down to Froghall where we turned round and came back, and then spent the evening in the Black Lion at Consall Forge, which is as isolated as you can get in Staffordshire. There was no mobile reception or TV or anything. We moored on the opposite bank from the pub, near the footbridge, where we spent the night. It was wonderfully peaceful and scenic (and there was no Royal Wedding news). Then we returned by the same route to Leek the next day. As I said, it was harder boating than I'd anticipated, and it made me realise just how much experience counts on the waterways. Helen assured me that she enjoyed it - apart from the locks. I tried to explain that locks were and are a part of boating, to be enjoyed as a chance to get off the boat, take in the scene, and chat to other boaters. But I think she remained a pilot rather than a boater, and probably always will.

After that we carried on with life in a similar fashion over the early summer, with Helen working part time and me taking care of odd things in the house; and both of us taking little trips...generally leading an ordinary life in fact. Then in late June we went on a big ship cruise together to the Northern Isles, Faroes, and Iceland. Helen had asked me several months earlier if I wanted to do this with her. We didn't know each other very well at the time, but she wanted to go and wasn't keen on paying a hefty single supplement. I'd never been on a cruise and wasn't sure if I'd like it, but I thought, "How bad can it be?" We seemed to get on well, and I realised that we'd find out, in a smallish cruise ship cabin, how well we actually got on. If we could get on well in that sort of environment for two weeks, then that would bode well for the future.

I left *LadyRiverMouse* on the visitor moorings in Endon, and Cookie stayed with my mother, since I wasn't too comfortable about leaving her with Maureen in Helen's house. Cookie had never met Maureen, and it might be a bit much for both of them! In spite of the initial trepidation we had a wonderful time, although we both decided that big ship cruising wasn't really for us. It just wasn't our sort of holiday...but that's another story.

I spent the rest of that summer similarly - pottering, visiting places in the Peak District, and gradually moving more and more stuff over to Helen's house. I still lived half on the boat and half in Helen's house, but I hadn't moved in completely. We spent more and more time together, but I still did a little bit of boating, mainly because I couldn't legally leave the boat in one place for longer than two weeks. I sailed the Caldon Canal several times between Leek, Endon, and Cheddleton - then back again. On one occasion, at Cheddleton, I met a guy who was cutting down trees with a chainsaw by the side of the canal. I said "That's an interesting job," and he replied "Do you want some wood?". "How much can I have", I asked. "How much do you want?", He replied. And he cut me logs for the boat. So you see I was still thinking like a boater. I wouldn't need logs in Helen's house as she had central heating, but I didn't think of that.

Chapter 15
Selling *LadyRiverMouse*:
the End of an Era.

In September 2011 I decided to take *LadyRiverMouse* to a marina. I realised that if things continued with my relationship with Helen as I now thought and hoped they would that I'd end up selling her, but I didn't want to dispose of my home just yet. After all, things still might go wrong. It was also going to take me a long time to move all my stuff off the boat if I was going to sell it. But *LadyRiverMouse* would be safer in a marina for the winter than parked by the side of the canal in Leek. So in late September Helen and I took my beloved *'Mouse'* down to the Marina in Kings Bromley. Helen was getting used to handling the boat by this time and it's a fairly easy trip, so although we had allowed a week we were there in only five days. I slowly transferred my relatively meagre belongings to Helen's house over the winter, as we had decided I was moving in – though I don't actually remember either of us making it a definite decision as such. So we made quite a few trips to the marina, removing a car full of my possessions each time.

I finally decided to put the boat on the market in March 2012. I had several brokers come and look at her, and give me estimates which varied from the ludicrous to the absolutely ridiculous as boat prices were suffering from the effects of the recession. In the end Nottingham Boat Sales seemed fairly reasonable, so I decided that she'd go to Nottingham to be sold. It turned out not to be a simple process, but we sold the boat and got the money eventually.

Therefore, at the end of March, Helen and I made our final trip in *LadyRiverMouse*, taking her to Nottingham. It was horrendous weather that week. Strong winds and teeming rain made boating difficult to say the least, but we were boating to a timetable; we had to be there on a certain day so we had to carry on. This is the worst sort of boating and is when accidents easily happen. If she wasn't already decided then I thought it was enough to put Helen off boating completely – although she did say afterwards that it really wasn't all that bad. I was just glad that it wasn't very far.

When we reached Nottingham we cleaned up *LadyRiverMouse,* then left her to be sold. It made me feel sad to leave her, but to be honest my feelings were very mixed. It was the end of a phase in my life - but life changes, and you move on. Sorrow was mixed with excitement - I was entering a new phase of my life, and life was getting better...

I was still pretty ill of course – at least, I'd been told I was. By this time I was on the strongest and final type of hormone therapy. It would only be effective for a few months at best, but I hadn't mentioned this to Helen, and I didn't know if she realised just how serious things had become. But - almost unbelievably - that changed too. Because I'd moved to Derbyshire, I changed my GP. Nothing much happened for a while, but eventually I phoned the new surgery and explained that I was supposed to have a hospital appointment. They made me an appointment for June 2012, but this time not in Birmingham where I'd been seen before, but in Derby, since this was closer. So I saw a new specialist, Dr Patel. I asked him the same question I'd asked the consultant in Birmingham so many times: "If this cancer has spread, then where is it?" Previously I'd just been told before that it didn't matter; it was all the same treatment anyway; just keep taking the medicine. But Dr Patel said, "I don't know, shall we find out?" So they started doing numerous scans and tests. I don't think there is a scan I didn't have: CT, MRI, Ultrasound, Nuclear Bone Density, X-rays - some of them more than once. Eventually I went back for the results, and he said, "I don't think this cancer has spread at all; I can't find it anywhere". Helen asked him if it could have spread initially and then gone away by itself, and he said that was in fact a possibility. Anyway, he thought maybe a course of radiotherapy would be very much to my advantage, as this is the usual treatment if the cancer is confined to the prostate. He said he would ask his team about this as he didn't want to take the decision alone, but he also asked me if I would want to have this treatment anyway; it was a long course with side effects, and he couldn't guarantee that it would work. But of course I said I would – any chance is better than no chance!

There were still more tests, scans, x-rays etc, but eventually a course of radiotherapy was arranged for me, for December 2012. That was quite a year, as in July 2012, Helen, who'd had arthritis in her knees for years, went into hospital to have both knee joints replaced. I looked after the cats during her stay, and I looked after her when she came home. I struggled a bit with all that as I'm not a natural nurse, but she was extremely grateful for what I managed to do. We seemed to have no sooner got over that when I had to start my 37 radiotherapy sessions, scheduled every weekday for several weeks. It was another hard winter, and on several days I couldn't even get the car out through the snow to get to Derby. These breaks didn't matter in medical terms, but it meant that the whole radiotherapy thing lasted from mid-December till the end of February 2013.

Finally it was all over, and the next time I had a test my PSA was falling dramatically. It takes a long time to drop, but it was going in the right direction. After a while they changed me from three monthly to six monthly checkups, and dropped some of the more nasty medications. So far all seemed to be well. And that is how things are today.

Chapter 16
2014 : An Update

At the time of writing (autumn 2014), Helen and I are still living happily together in her house. It is now in a good state of repair, and even the former jungle of a garden is beginning to look good. Helen still does quite a bit of writing, and as you can see from this book, she's now got me doing it too – no, it wasn't ghost written; although I've appreciated the guidance and editing. Helen made an excellent recovery from her knee operation, and is far more active than she was before she had it done. So we walk, swim, do yoga, have taken up ballroom dancing, and are cat care volunteers at the local Cats Protection adoption centre. We take regular holidays to foreign countries, but interestingly enough, very rarely on boats.

Cookie, now aged 17, is still with us, spending more and more time on her heating pad and less and less time exploring the house. She seems very pleased to have somewhere to live in her old age which is warm and doesn't move about. She is finally beginning to get on with the other cats, though she still has her own room, food bowls, and litter tray and will have until the day she is no longer with us. Our much-loved Persian, Gizmo, died a year ago at the age of sixteen and a half, and he was followed by Cavi about six months later; he had inoperable cancer. We are considering getting a new kitten, but not while Cookie is alive as it simply wouldn't be fair on her.

Josh got his degree and is now living happily in Oxford. Lizzie and her partner came back from Ireland, and now live about an hour's journey from us. My mother and my sister Diane, who both feature briefly in this book, are both well. And my test results continue to look good.

Overall, the future looks bright – especially as I never expected to have a future at all by this time. It's a funny old life, when you look at it overall. It was only because of a catalogue of disasters in my life that I was able to fulfil my dream of living on a boat on the canals. And it was only my meeting Helen and subsequently changing hospitals that led to my improved state of health. It's been a bit of a rocky ride but I will always be grateful that things worked out in the way they did.

Appendix
A Day in the Life of a Narrowboater

The sun has already come up and it's light in the cabin when I am awoken by the gentle touch of a fluffy white paw and the not quite so gentle rasping of a rough tongue. Cookie is awake and would rather like breakfast.

There's a chill in the cabin, although the solid fuel stove still has a glimmer of life and will soon burst into activity, with a little more fuel and a rake of the ashes. Then it's on with the kettle, before filling a dish for Cookie and making breakfast for myself. Toast is difficult as there is not enough electrical power for a toaster and the little grill on the stove gives a very variable heat – burning one end of the slice while leaving the other end untouched. Judicious turning of bread slices will give an even finish but it's a bit of an art. No power for a microwave either, so my scrambled egg is done in the traditional old fashioned way, with a saucepan.

A quick trip to the shower room. No bath on the boat; there is not enough water in the tank to fill one even if I could find the space. My fears of the previous night are confirmed – the effluent tank is almost full. It will need emptying today...

Back in the kitchen a light on the fridge is blinking at me. During the night the fridge has run

LadyRiverMouse's battery down and the light is warning me of that fact. It's time to start the engine to replenish the charge and to heat the hot water for a shower later. It will take at least two hours to get any meaningful charge into the battery; four hours would be better, but I'm mindful of running the engine in the evening as it upsets local residents, both water and land dwelling.

The trip to the local boatyard to get the effluent tank emptied will take me across to the other side of town through a swing bridge and a lock. It's not very far – 10 minutes to walk - it but will take me around an hour. The first problem is that *LadyRiverMouse* is facing in the wrong direction. The waterway is not wide enough to turn a 50 foot boat, so I need to go about half a mile in the wrong direction before I find a place where a river enters the canal and there is enough width of water to turn around – or 'wind' as it is technically termed. Pronounced as in the air that blows, not as in wind the handle.

Turning a narrowboat is a bit of an art in itself. The technique is to steer the bows into the winding hole (as the wide bit of water is known) and then use the engine to push the stern around. It helps if the wind (that blows) is behind you to assist with this turning. If not, then as a last resort it is possible to ram the bow gently into the soft bank to hold it so that the rest of the boat pirouettes slowly round. As an added complication winding holes have an almost magnetic attraction for anglers, who hate boats using them for their intended purpose; so during the fishing season the whole manoeuvre can be accompanied by loud cursing from the bank. Wise boaters ignore this and carry on regardless. I don't think I've ever met a happy angler, which makes me wonder why they do it if it makes them so miserable.

Having got *LadyRiverMouse* at least facing in the right direction, it is about three quarters of a mile back past our original mooring to the point where a swing bridge bars the way. The bridge carries a minor road and is boater friendly in that the controls are on the towpath side. This is not always the case and leads to all sorts of complications – see chapter 4. The bridge is also electrically powered, which saves a lot of physical effort, but the barriers to the road are manually swung, as is normal. I moor just before the bridge and - remembering to take my British Waterways key with me - I walk up to the bridge. There is very little vehicular traffic but a fair few walkers as this is a popular route into town, and I try to wait for a gap before closing the barriers. I have to be careful to get both barriers firmly locked as there is a fail safe system and the bridge will not operate if a barrier is unlocked. Then as quickly as possible I insert my key into the control panel and press the 'open bridge' button. It takes a while for the mechanism to start but eventually the bridge starts to move. When the bridge is fully open I can return to *LadyRiverMouse*, untie the mooring ropes, move the short distance to the other side of the bridge, tie up again, and return to the control panel to close the bridge and remove my key. By this time a fair crowd of people will have amassed on both sides, and maybe a car or two. I never encountered any impatience; it seems that people are only too willing to watch the boats go by.

It is only a couple of hundred yards to the next obstacle – a lock. The earliest canals avoided locks by hugging the contours of the land, and were indeed known as contour canals. This couldn't last, and eventually someone had to design a method of getting canals up and down hills. Many things have been tried but the simplest and most common by far is the lock. Put simply, a section of canal is isolated by two sets of gates, set just over a boat length apart, which close across the waterway. This allows the water between the gates to be raised or lowered, carrying a boat up or down with it. The water level is controlled by large taps known as 'paddles', and when the desired level is achieved the gates can be opened and the boat driven in or out. Simple technology but as always dangers lurk...

The lock in front of me now is a wide lock and I am going down to a lower level, which means that I will end up on a lower section of canal than I started on.. A wide lock will take two narrowboats side by side if necessary. The first thing to do is to tie *LadyRiverMouse* to the lock moorings – a set of bollards provided for the purpose. Then I walk to the lock, this time taking my windlass with me – an L shaped spanner for turning the mechanism that will open and close the paddles. As is normal the lock is half full when I start. They leak a bit so this is a sort of equilibrium for any lock left for a while. I will need to completely fill it before I can open the top gates to allow *LadyRiverMouse* to enter. This I do by opening the paddles in or by the top gates. Water rushes in and before long the lock is full. The weight of water is such that no matter how hard I lean on the long lever or balance beam that opens the gate it will not move until the water levels are exactly equal. As this is a wide lock there are two gates at the top and bottom but I only have to open one of them.

Once this is done I can return to

LadyRiverMouse, untie the mooring lines, and drive her into the lock. Then it is a matter of closing the top gate, and opening the bottom paddles to let the water out of the lock chamber. I must not forget to close the top paddles, which I opened earlier, and to take a rope ashore to control the boat as she drops along with the falling water level.

During this process invariably a crowd of 'gongoozlers' arrives. These are canal onlookers; they are not a problem as such, but it is important not to get distracted by folk asking questions as I need to keep an eye on the emptying lock for potential problems. Ropes snag and people throw all sorts of things into locks, any of which could cause a problem and require some very rapid paddle closing.

When the lock is empty it is possible to open the bottom gate; then I get back on board to drive the boat out of the lock. The boat is of course now eight feet below the lock side so getting back on board entails climbing down a wet weed-encrusted iron ladder set into the lock side, while at the same time making sure that the boat stays still with a rope looped round a bollard in such a way that it can be retrieved from below. No problem at all then... Of course if there are two of you then one can stay on board, eliminating this rather tricky step. In fact, having two people aboard cuts down the work at locks by about two-thirds. Finally it is a simple matter of driving out of the lock, mooring up yet again, and walking back to make sure all the gates and paddles are closed, before continuing on your merry way.

I need to go another half mile to the service dock of the local boatyard. This is a reserved mooring, kept just for boaters requiring all the services that I now need. While I'm waiting for Joe, the chap who runs the place, I run out a hose to an adjacent standpipe and start to fill *LadyRiverMouse's* water tank. The tank is huge, holding around 1000 litres, which means that I never run out of water (I never did in all my time of boating); but I still like to top up at every convenient point. Also there are the bags of rubbish to be disposed of in the skip. Like everyone else in the modern world I always seem to be filling empty bin bags, which have to be stored until an opportunity arises to throw them away. At this point Cookie takes a look outside. She knows this boatyard well and is only too aware that it has its own shore cat who guards his territory ferociously. She takes a sniff of the air and wisely goes back to her place on my armchair.

Soon Joe appears from his little office and starts the pump-out procedure. A large vacuum hose is attached to a fitting on *LadyRiverMouse,* and a hidden machine sucks the effluent from the tank on board. Joe prides himself on providing the best pump-out on the system and gently rocks '*Mouse* from side to side with his foot as the machine slurps away. This helps prevent sediment building up in the tank. When the tank is nearly empty he gives me the nod and I empty several buckets of canal water down the loo. This flushes the system through and helps prevent blockages in the future. These systems are notoriously intolerant of things like quilted toilet paper and therefore I only ever use the thin cheap stuff which seems to give no problems.

While we are doing this I notice that Joe has a good offer on diesel. *LadyRiverMouse* doesn't have a fuel gauge so I dip the tank to see how much I can get in. The tank hold around 250 litres and I never let it fall below a third full. This helps prevent sediment getting drawn into the engine which would mean a certain breakdown. On this occasion I work out that there is room for about 80 litres – well worth filling up at the price offered.

All done, we retire to Joe's little office to work out how much I owe. We have to calculate the tax due on the quantity of diesel that I will use to move the boat. I need to pay tax on that amount, but the diesel used for domestic things like battery charging and heating the hot water is tax free. There is no set way of calculating this and I have my own system, keeping a log of engine hours in a little notebook. By consulting this I come up with a percentage on which I have to pay tax, and then Joe does the sums. I pay my bill; with the pump-out and fuel it is approaching three figures. Then I head back to the boat for a spot of lunch, before retracing my steps back to my overnight mooring.

I spend a couple of hours tidying up the boat; living in a small area means that it's important to keep everything in its place. I then polish some of the brasswork, a job I like to keep on top of. Later that afternoon I put the oven on to cook my dinner, only for the flame to flicker and die. The gas has run out. It is an unwritten rule of boating that the gas will expire just after a boatyard visit – and always in the middle of cooking something. No problem as I have a spare cylinder, I just need to go out on the tiny foredeck and reach into the gas locker with a spanner. The new bottle will last a couple of months – plenty of time to get a replacement for the empty cylinder.

As darkness draws in I trim and fill the oil lamps I use for light in the cabin. *LadyRiverMouse* does have electric light, but using the oil lamps helps conserve the battery power for more important things like surfing the internet on my little netbook or watching TV on the tiny 8" set that I bought solely for it's low power consumption. However, if there is anything that I want to watch I'll have to put the aerial up first; I can't travel with it in position as it's too tall for the bridges. I'll also need to see to the solid fuel stove which provides most of the heating. *LadyRiverMouse* does have a gas boiler and radiators, but it uses an extraordinary amount of bottled gas. I once emptied a bottle of gas in three days, so I only use it in emergencies.

Time for a quick shower before bed. *LadyRiverMouse's* shower is, how can I put this...an experience. The water is supplied to the shower head by the on-board pumps. There are two - one for the hot and one for the cold. The problem is that they deliver the water in pulses, and they tend to get out of phase so that one pulse is of cold, and the next of hot, rather than keeping to a steady temperature. The cold is at canal temperature (ie very cold) as it has been kept in the tank in the bottom of the boat; the hot is scalding as it has been heated by the engine for four hours - around 80C, or 15-20 degrees hotter than a domestic house hot water system. As if that weren't enough, the shower tray is emptied by a very noisy pump which discharges the soapy water out into the canal. This pump is powerful enough to grab an unwary foot and suck it on to the drain. The pump switch is just out of reach when you're using the shower. So for the unwary there is the scenario of being alternately frozen and scalded, while trapped by the foot with the release switch just out of reach, and unable to shout for help over the noise of the pump! Luckily experience has taught me to turn hot and cold taps fully on, which stops the pulsing, and to keep my feet well away from the drain hole.

And so we turn in for the night, me on the permanent bed in the back cabin and Cookie on my armchair. She will try to get on my bed during the night; and probably succeed, as she usually does. After a busy day's boating, which finished exactly where we had started that morning, we both sleep extraordinarily well.

LadyRiverMouse in a wide lock. Note the closed doors to keep Cookie safely inside

About the Authors

David Thomas was born in the depths of the English Midlands. After a chaotic schooling he spent 22 years working for British Telecom, finally becoming Network Planning Manager. Tiring of the rat race, he left and started his own children's nursery, which he ran for 20 years. He lived in Spain for a short period, before returning to the UK to begin the epic waterways journey which is the subject of this book. In 2010 he met Helen, and they have been together ever since. He enjoys gardening, building model boats, and of course spending time with his beloved cat Cookie. "Travels with Cookie" is his first book, and he found writing it harder than he expected.

Helen Krasner was born in Croydon; then lived in Edinburgh, California, and North Wales, before moving to the Derbyshire Peak District around nine years ago. She has had a somewhat chequered career, working among other things as an occupational psychologist, meditation teacher, and market research consultant/report writer. In her 40s she learned to fly; then became a helicopter instructor. For the last few years she has earned her living as a writer, and has published several books and numerous articles. Since meeting David she has lived with him in her house, along with her three cats and the eponymous Cookie. "Travels with Cookie" was her brainchild, since she felt David had a story which needed to be told.

Helen and David on holiday in Iceland

Helen's cat Magnus who replied so splendidly to Cookie's pleadings on the Soulmates site for a new friend for her boss.

Final Note

If you have enjoyed this book, you might like one of Helen Krasner's other books. "Midges, Maps & Muesli" is an account of a a record breaking 5,000 mile walk around the coast of Britain, which she undertook in the 1980s. It is available on Amazon, in both print and ebook versions. This is how it starts:

Chapter 1 - Preparations: The Best Laid Plans...

I was lost. I didn't want to believe it, but it was true. The fog had come down suddenly, as often happens on the coast, and it had caught me completely unawares. I could hardly see a yard in front of me, and I had no idea where to go or what to do. I had tried to find my way by compass bearing but it had been no use. For I had lost the footpath when the fog first descended; and with hedges, fences and impenetrable scrub, not to mention a hundred foot drop to the sea somewhere off to my left, I hardly dared move, let alone cut cross-country. Anyway, I reminded myself dismally, I didn't really have much idea how to take a compass bearing. I'd planned to go on a navigation course before starting this walk, but it had been one of the many things I'd meant to do but hadn't— along with training, planning the route, listening to weather forecasts. None of it had actually happened.

I wasn't really afraid, or so I tried to tell myself anyway, and I almost believed it. Actually I felt rather stupid. For while I had expected to get lost at some point on a 5,000 mile walk around the coast of Britain, I had assumed it would be in the Scottish Highlands, on the North Cornish coast, or in some other wild, desolate corner of the country. But no, here I was, on only my tenth day of the walk, a couple of miles from Swanage in Dorset, on a path walked by thousands of tourists every year. I was so close to the town I could hear the traffic in the streets and a cow mooing in a nearly farm. But I might as well have been a thousand miles away for all the good it did me.

As the damp, impenetrable mist swirled around me I took a couple of deep breaths and tried to decide what to do. Well, I thought to myself, trying hard to be rational, I had a tent, a sleeping bag, and enough food. I could survive even if I had to spend the night up there. There was no reason to panic; getting lost wasn't a disaster. Something of the sort had to happen sometime. Anyway, I was a tough, experienced long distance walker, super-fit and entirely confident of my ability to walk right round the coast of Britain safely. Wasn't I?

The answer was no, I wasn't. I was an ordinary woman with time on her hands and a romantic idea, and not much else. And there was no doubt about it now, I was beginning to get scared. It was true that I had enough equipment to spend the night in the hills if necessary, but logic doesn't help much in these situations. It didn't alter the fact that I was cold, lonely, and miserable. I wanted to go home, to sit by the fire and the TV like sane, normal people.

"Why?" I asked myself for the hundredth time in five minutes. Why, why, why had I got myself into this situation? I knew I should have seen the fog coming. Clearly, I thought to myself, I didn't have the knowledge or experience for this sort of walk. I should never have begun it in the first place.

'It's all Miriam's fault," I muttered to myself, quite irrationally, and entirely unfairly. "She started all this. It was her idea."

This wasn't true and I knew it, but it helped a bit to have someone else to blame. Though my old friend Miriam had indeed played a part in it. Had it really been only a few months ago?

-o-

Helen has also written several book on aviation, both print and ebooks, plus ebooks on other topics. Again, all of these can be found on Amazon.

Printed in Great Britain
by Amazon.co.uk, Ltd.,
Marston Gate.